Survival in groups
The basics of group membership

Survival in groups

The basics of group membership

TOM DOUGLAS

Open University Press
Buckingham • Philadelphia

Open University Press
Celtic Court
22 Ballmoor
Buckingham
MK18 1XW

and 1900 Frost Road, Suite 101
Bristol, PA 19007, USA

First published 1995

A catalogue record of this book is available from the British Library

ISBN   0 335 19413 3 (hb)   0 335 19412 5 (pb)

Library of Congress Cataloging-in-Publication Data
Douglas, Tom.
    Survival in groups : the basics of group membership / Tom Douglas.
        p.   cm.
    Includes bibliographical references (p.   ) and index.
    ISBN 0–335–19413–3 (hb), — ISBN 0–335–19412–5 (pb)
    1. Small groups.   2. Collective behavior.   I. Title.
HM133.D69 1995
302.3′4—dc20   95–15367
                                                            CIP

Typeset by Graphicraft Typesetters Limited, Hong Kong
Printed in Great Britain by Biddles Limited, Guildford and King's Lynn

To Shirley with love as always

and

to those students who told me
that they wanted to be good
group members rather than group
leaders.

Contents

1 The book: aims, bases and uses

Aims: general aims of the book, and a look at some of the basic confusions about groups
Bases: where the source material of the book came from
Uses: how the contents of this book can be used to the best advantage

---

Aims

This chapter aims to provide information about groups which is relevant to any understanding about working in and with groups. It is intended to state clearly what the book aims to achieve by examining groups and the way they function, not from the point of view of the group leader but from that of the group member. It also aims to show where the material which is used here came from and the reasons why it was selected for inclusion and, finally, it gives some hints as to how the best use may be made of it.

> **Aim 1**
> The primary aim is to show that the experience of being a member of a group, which is common to all of us, can become the basis of a learning programme for developing informed and proficient group membership skills.

There is no mystery about groups. Indeed, it is absolutely true to say that being a member of a group is one of the most universally common experiences of all human beings. The problem is that when something is so common, few of us bother to take much notice of it and take it for granted. So when for various reasons it becomes necessary to examine what goes on in groups in order to be able to create groups for special purposes, the complex analyses which emerge tend to generate a mystification process about something which we all thought was a common and everyday experience.

One of the first aims of this book is to try to put ideas about groups back where they belong, in the realm of common experience:

> **Aim 2**
> To demystify the ideas about groups and return them to common experience.

In the process, I hope that we will also be able to add something which at this stage I will simply call 'structure'. By this I mean that we will endeavour to give to the common knowledge about groups an order and organization which will allow individuals to use that knowledge much more effectively in their roles as members of various groups.

This leads directly to the second aim of this book, which is to enable individuals to know what it is they already know about groups and, more importantly, what it is that they do not as yet know and thus what it is that they might need to learn.

> **Aim 3**
> Another aim is to highlight what each individual may already know about being a member of a group, to organize that knowledge and also to find out what else needs to be learned.

In his book *Stalking the Wild Pendulum*, Itzhak Bentov wrote that '. . . one's level of ignorance increases exponentially with accumulated knowledge'. What he was saying in a very concise way was that as one acquires knowledge, each new addition to the store generates many questions and, as the generation of questions is many times greater than the acquisition of knowledge, 'The more one knows, therefore, the greater the level of his ignorance'.

This is not as depressing as it sounds, for what it means in very ordinary language is that there is usually a great deal more to any area of study than at first appears. Thus the wholly enjoyable process of learning once embarked upon is never ending.

I have been working with, learning and teaching about groups for about forty years and, although I now know a great deal more about groups and groupwork than I did when I began, I am also aware of the vast amount which there is to know. So what is at issue here is not just learning about being a member of a group or endeavouring to encompass most of the available knowledge, but rather coming to grips with those areas of information about groups and being a member of a group which will enable us, in very practical ways, to have greater control over the group decisions we are involved with and to understand better the possible consequences.

Basic confusion

Although most people live and work in what might be described as a 'group' situation, what emerges with startling clarity when they start to discuss this fact is that while they would agree that they live and work in the company of other people, there is a fundamental uncertainty as to whether these small human gatherings are truly to be seen as 'groups'. Thus any teaching and reading about groups tends to be imposed upon a basic confusion about what groups actually are or are not, and so people struggle to make the mental leap from everyday experience to highly sophisticated and very partisan concepts such as encounter groups. This is like expecting people to read Latin texts before gaining even a rudimentary smattering of grammar and vocabulary. The result as ever is that what is achieved by dint of hard labour and gritty determination at the sophisticated end rests on a very shaky foundation. This is not a good outcome, because the manner of achieving it makes it very inflexible. If there is little understanding of the essential sources from which the complex ideas grew, then they can only be operated as a routine with no flexibility, capacity or understanding to meet situations which do not fit that routine in a very narrow and precise way.

From this fact springs one of the basic criticisms of all attempts to understand and utilize a knowledge of human behaviour. It is that the variety of human behaviour is squashed into rigidly defined pigeon-holes with which one is familiar, and thus the application of understanding is therefore much less related to individual need than it is to the rigid and restricted knowledge base of the user. Which, in somewhat simpler terms, can be stated as another aim of this book:

Aim 4

To clarify what is meant by the term 'group' in various contexts and thus be able to demonstrate that all human beings have an extremely wide, various and continuous experience of groups which can be made usable by being made visible and organized, becoming the basis of a well-founded and flexible understanding of group behaviour.

Following on from this, another can be stated which is to show simple methods by which the personal experience of both past and present can be turned into useful knowledge.

Working with groups – that is, as a member – is essentially a practical skill but one in which each individual has to adapt the known general understandings of group behaviour to the kind of person they are and the kind of group situations in which they operate. Thus although much basic understanding can and must come from books, discussion, watching, etc., the ultimate hurdle is how that information can be used by the individual in appropriate and successful ways.

Every educationist is aware that the gap between knowing and successful doing can be dauntingly difficult to bridge. For this reason, each major aspect of working with groups dealt with in this book must be accompanied by some attempt on the part of the reader, however limited, to put it into useful practice. Most learners will be offered few opportunities to receive skilled supervision in this difficult transition and so it is essential that circumstances should be created in which two important learning devices can be brought into play: *discussion* and *feedback*. Much more will be said about these later and the techniques of their use elaborated upon. Few people to my knowledge have become competent in the skills of working with groups who have not discussed their performances within groups with others, whether skilled groupworkers or not, or who have not received feedback on their performances from others in the group or from those closely associated with it.

> Any individual working with groups can only become proficient by receiving feedback on his or her performance, which is then used to upgrade that performance.

Incidentally, when groups go drastically wrong, there is often a kind of post-mortem to discover if possible the causes of failure. While this may be a necessary procedure, it can also be a dangerous one when the examination of those causes turns to the allocation of blame. Of course, some group members may bear a greater responsibility for the dismal group outcome than others. But accusations of blame are only justified if they produce an agreement about causes, and, if the group is to continue to exist, ways and means to prevent such an event occurring again. Some of this process will be illuminated further when we look at the ways in which groups tend to preserve themselves by laying their mistakes on the shoulders of one or more selected group members or outsiders.

> Group failures present the opportunity for development towards more effective functioning if blame-laying processes are not allowed to become destructive.

The other side of the discussion of failure is the analysis of success. It is a strange fact that in all the years I have been working with groups and groupworkers, rarely have the participants in an effective group voluntarily suggested that they should consider what contributed to their success. It is almost as if they believed that success should not be questioned; maybe because to do so would somehow detract from their satisfaction. But the question, 'If this worked so well, don't you want to know why?', should always be asked and if possible answered.

Admittedly, there is more point to asking such a question than in actually discovering the causes of success, valuable as they might prove to be. But what will emerge is that each and every member of a successful group will have some different explanation for that success, though many will have some degree of overlap. Of course, they may all be right. Equally, the differences will be very illuminating, if only to demonstrate an essential truth about human behaviour, which is that we are seldom in total agreement about the explanation of outcomes. As we shall see later, differences are not necessarily oppositions; indeed, as we shall also have to make very plain, difference is actually the essential and basic resource in the way groups work.

> All reviews of group performance should concentrate equally on success and failure.

When an analysis of successful group performance reveals why it occurred, then there is the beginning of a new kind of practical understanding which is seldom even referred to in textbooks. The logic of it goes something like this:

1. This group was successful (in achieving what it set out to do).
2. Why was this so?
3. Several factors are thought likely to be responsible (after discussion and the scanning of such records of the life of the group as are available).
4. What can be learned from this analysis?
   (a) That in this kind of group (i.e. similar members, task, constraints), these factors will tend to produce a good outcome.
   (b) That in similar situations (see above), they may therefore be applied consciously but with appropriate modification for known difference to produce the required outcome.

It is only by such a procedure that the techniques of group management and survival become the knowledge and possession of individuals, adapted to their individual personality and not the off-the-shelf techniques of writers and others.

It must be remembered that the techniques of experienced workers, though fascinating when demonstrated for use, automatically lack one of their most essential ingredients of successful application for anyone else – the individual personality and presence of the original user.

> Theoretical techniques of working with groups are always modified in practice by the personality, presence and experience of the person using them.

Frequently, when starting work with a number of individuals who are interested in learning about groups, I ask them: 'What do you think you already know about groups?' This is a very open question; in fact, it is so open that many people find difficulty in knowing where to start. Try it. Take a pen and a sheet of paper and write down your response to this question.

Exercise

A very good place to start is to list all the groups of which you have been, and in some cases still are, a member. Include family, friendship groups, work groups, leisure groups, clubs, special interest gatherings, political and religious groups, etc. Having done this, then try to record what you think you may have learned from your membership of such groups. When this is as complete as you can make it, consider it carefully. I expect that you may find that certain kinds of learning from your experience which you have noted show marked signs of having a great deal in common (e.g. you may have noted several times that large groups are more comfortable to be in than small ones; that in some groups it is easy to make oneself heard and in others almost impossible, and so on). So the next task in this small exercise is to collect together the similar responses so that the information derived from your experiences becomes ordered into compartments and therefore useful. The final task is to make a quick primary assessment of where your information is plentiful and strong and to make some inspired guesses at what areas appear bare or non-existent.

The difference between structured (i.e. organized) knowledge and knowledge which has been duly collected but not yet structured, can be illustrated using the analogy of a library and a second-hand bookshop. In the former, everything is classified in several different ways so that whatever information you start with, there is a route available to you to find what you want. There is also a system that can tell you not only whether what you want is available, but what may have happened to it if it is not. In the second-hand bookshop, unless it is organized along the lines of a library, the assistant may know that what you want is there but not know where to find it or anything else about it without an extensive search.

> Knowledge and information which are structured and organized are available for immediate use. It is usually also immediately apparent in a structured system what is not available.

It is just as important to know where the gaps are in your knowledge and experience as to know in an organized way what you do know.

Most texts on working in and with groups are aimed at those who expect to create or adapt existing groups to meet specially selected needs and to pursue defined outcomes. But it is obvious on reflection that all people are much more likely to find themselves members of more groups than they will find themselves leaders. Also, it has become apparent that while we glibly assert that group experience is universal, we overlook the fact that the creation of groups for specific purposes (i.e. for purposes other than those which are normally found in our society and in which most of us had our formative experiences of groups) is regarded by many as a highly artificial and thus suspect procedure. Thus it becomes necessary, in some measure, not only to prepare people for member-ship of these groups which tend to be regarded as artificial, but also to begin the process of demonstrating their value to the potential membership. Thus another important aim of this book is to present information about groups from the point of view of the group member. All group members have responsibility for what happens in a group and all group members should be able, having the knowledge and skill, to influence group outcomes should they choose to do so.

> **Aim 5**
> A major aim of this book is to present information about working in groups from the point of view of being a group member.

Bases

By 'bases' I mean the sources of the material presented here. It may seem wholly unnecessary to offer this information to the reader, who may well as-sume that as long as he or she finds the material interesting and useful, then where it comes from is not his or her concern. But it is! In working in groups in any shape or form, it is as well to remember that credibility plays an enor-mous part. Let us digress for a moment in order to elaborate upon this point and consider the general question of perception.

Simply stated, what we know of ourselves and others and of the world in which we live derives from our sensory perceptions, what we see, feel, hear, smell, sense, etc. But sensory perceptions are not an automatic recording system like a thermomenter, but have an end-product which is essentially individual, largely learned, variable and idiosyncratic. In a word, whatever the similarity of the sensory inputs we receive may be, we tend to interpret them in ways we have developed as we grew. Thus, for instance, if we ask several people to name the colour of a piece of material in the same light and at the same instant so that the incoming wavelength is as near identical for everyone as it is possible to be, the answers given will be very different because each individual has learned to describe that particular effect of light stimulus in a particular way.

How much more difference should we expect when what is being assessed is not just a simple colour perception but a complex pattern of behaviour? The answer is a great deal. The point is that we live in a world of individual percep-tions where similarities and differences occur. Let us now return first of all to credibility and, second, to the sources of the material presented here.

In a group where people are working together to achieve stated ends, it becomes necessary to invest some degree of interest and commitment in the group unless one is to be just a passenger and a net consumer of group energy rather than a net contributor. But such an investment of energy, interest and commitment is never risk-free. And so a very simple equation arises, which results in the level of commitment being compatible in the individual member's view with the amount of risk he or she sees as being involved. Of course, this is not to say that the perception of risk is an accurate one. Indeed, one of the changes which occurs in group members as their length of membership increases is a different calculation of the risk to which they are exposed. In a simpler form, this is often described as the degree of trust that exists within the group, which in effect is calculated as how secure and safe the member feels.

The interesting point here is that different individuals have highly different perceptions both of the safety of the group in which they are a member and of the amount of trust they place in it. One of the major functions of a group is that, if it continues to exist over a period of time, members' opinions of risks, trust and commitment change. Why? Well simply because they have had time to see for themselves during their membership of the group how it actually deals with its members.

I once asked a fairly experienced groupworker why he hadn't intervened in a staff group to prevent it taking what turned out later to have been a disastrous decision. His reply was illuminating:

'There is no way', he said, 'that I could have intervened in that group at that time despite the fact I thought I could see what was likely to happen'.

'Why not?', I asked.

'For the simple reason that over the weeks that I have been in this group, I have seen several demonstrations of the way that they treat relative newcomers who make critical comment. It was not encouraging'.

There are at least two points of learning here. First, the staff member had recognized very clearly the limits of his credibility with his colleagues and, second, being a relatively new member of the staff group, he only had evidence of the way that untrusted new members were treated and none of how the situation could develop later. Indeed, this was a situation of minimal trust based upon minimal knowledge of each of the parties involved.

Credibility is generated by the accumulation of evidence over time, but in presenting material in a book like this that kind of development of credibility is not possible. As one of the least trustworthy statements ever made by one human being to another is the request 'trust me', it is necessary to offer a different kind of credibility.

The material offered here has been derived from many workshops held over some thirty years with people whose interest in groups and groupwork has been an essential point of their working lives. Some came with a considerable theoretical knowledge of groups derived from professional training courses and wide reading. Others had found themselves, almost without benefit of either training or reading, thrust into a work situation in which working with groups, being a member of a staff group, etc., was an integral part.

These people, then, have come to workshops, asked questions, presented problems and generated a mass of information not so much *about* groups, but how to survive in a positive way in groups by being more aware of what is going on. This is a very pragmatic approach. Information and knowledge has to be translated into plans for actual members within actual groups, which means that if nothing else it is information that can be used by workshop members. Three very important factors emerge from this:

1. Theoretical ideas derived from research have widely different values in actual application and at best can only provide wide general guidance.
2. The language of theory is inappropriate in the development of methods and techniques of being an effective group member.
3. The need for supervision, or at least the opportunity to discuss what one is doing, is essential for development.

Point 3 will be dealt with in greater detail in Chapter 9. Suffice it to say here that feedback from others about how one is performing is essential. The gap between knowing and doing is a wide one and quite daunting to attempt to bridge alone. Putting ideas into action, and using information deliberately and consciously, requires monitoring for effect.

To sum up, the material presented here is derived from and based upon the work of many people involved with groups and is, I hope, couched in language which has been found to be useful in that context. The information presented is that which these people have found practical and useful in application. So although a great deal may be missing, what is here should cover the basic necessities of working in groups.

Uses

I indicate here the way that the rest of the book is laid out and suggest the best way of making use of the material.

There are four principal sections: First, Chapter 1 sets out the aims of the book. It presents information about being a member of a group and about groups in general, and what the material is based upon, and ends by suggesting how the material presented can be used to the best advantage by the reader. Next, Chapters 2–5 spell out what we mean when we talk about 'groups' by demonstrating all those factors which groups have in common and highlighting the most prominent differences. These chapters also go some way to explaining how and why groups function. Then, Chapters 6–9 attempt to show how the knowledge of groups presented in Chapters 1–5 can be used to facilitate being in and working with groups and eventually help the development of the skill not only of positive survival in groups, but also the ability to affect group outcomes deliberately and by design. Finally, Chapter 10 presents the possibility of monitoring all the foregoing material and the actions of the individual group member/reader, and of combining them into a coherent structure of knowledge and practice which can then become the basis upon which further learning and skill can be founded as desired. There is also a short reading list.

It is essential that as often as possible, you, the reader, should try to relate what you read to your own individual experience. Groups are no places for people with undigested and unintegrated theoretical concepts of group behaviour. When, for instance, you read about a new entrant into an already existing group or an individual who comes to work in a group care residential establishment, you must run through in your own mind any experience you have which is similar and then run the experience and the reading side by side. Reading a book such as this from cover to cover at one sitting will avail most readers little. It is essentially a *work book of group membership skills* and each and every part needs to be related and closely tied to the actuality of your experience if this is at all possible.

If you do not currently have the experience to relate to what you read, then it will no doubt come later. The point is that working in groups is essentially a practical activity and fundamentally tied to who the individual group member is and the situations in which he or she operates. If you can use the information given here and adapt it so that it is compatible with you as a person, then we are in business.

Finally, a number of points about using a book like this need to be clearly stated:

1. No-one ever became a competent group member or leader by only reading books.
2. Because this is so obviously true, learning about groups and group membership should not be a passive undertaking. It is essential that whenever the reader recognizes something in the text which bears a resemblance to his or her own group circumstances, a conscious effort should be made to take the information here and apply it to real situations.

> You must try out relevant ideas and see what happens. Even a 'good' idea may not work for you, although it works very well for others.

3. Talk to your colleagues about the ideas you are trying to develop into techniques or into enhanced understanding. But remember different people see the same things differently.
4. Use Chapter 10 to provide you with ideas of how to proceed. Life in groups doesn't just flow like water in a river – various pressures are exerted inside and outside to make it go in selected directions. You must learn to be active both as regards recognition and intervention. Learn to change gear and to make deliberate and conscious choices of what you want to do, but be careful to found these on a recognition of what is already happening and what the possible consequences may be. Remember also that in all forms of social intervention, the most important consequences tend to be those which were unforeseen.

> If you don't recognize what is happening in your group, then your choice of action or understanding is likely to be severely limited.

I have tried to set out clearly what it is that those who work with groups think is important to know about groups and the ways in which people behave in them. Once this information has become part of your understanding, then there is nothing to stop you reading anything that takes your interest about groups and groupwork, for you should by then have a good sound basis upon which to judge the quality and usefulness of what you read. You should also have developed a yardstick for recognizing the value of information and of testing it in practice to see whether it suits the way you want to learn or operate.

It must be understood that almost all human existence takes place in the context of groups of one sort or another. For example, various caring roles and procedures must be seen to encompass both the carers and those who are cared for, usually in group situations. Here the behaviours of each are visible to others and support, guidance and other responses are conditioned as much by being a member of a group as by being an individual occupying a caring or receiving role. It is therefore essential that all carers should be aware of the influence that the group dimension can have on their work, both from the members of the group receiving care and the members of the group giving care. They should begin to understand how the influences (the dynamics) of such groups, however weak or loosely structured they may be, or however lightly membership is held in them, will affect their daily work. Of course, some carers will actively work with groups that have been created deliberately. In such cases, a good basic understanding of groups is even more necessary. Most carers will be part of a team working within a particular environment and teams are a particular form of group structure.

Finally, any additional knowledge of group processes is invaluable for an understanding of the pressures which arise among ordinary groupings of family and friends, and open up the possibility of a choice of actions for those involved based upon a rational insight into the forces at work.

Summary of main points

1. The basis for developing sound group membership skill is to be found in structured and organized group experiences which are common to everyone.
2. The foundation of learning about groups is based upon a thorough review of what one already knows from one's own personal experience.
3. Theoretical ideas about group behaviour need to be translated into practical understanding for those who work in groups and to be compatible with the individuals who use them.

4. Learning is an active process and ideas need to be tried out in real-life situations.

List of basic concepts and terms

1. *Self-learning programme*: the need to be disciplined and active. No social skill like effective group membership can be learnt solely from a book. It is necessary to test and try out, to analyse, record and assess, to talk to others, to compare and to listen.
2. *Structure of knowledge*: information is organized in such a way that each area's relationship to all the others is clearly shown, and their influences on one another are visible.
3. *Credibility*: being seen and accepted by others as a person of value and worth either generally or in some specific situation based on the apparent possession of appropriate knowledge, skill, power, understanding, etc.
4. *Feedback*: receiving some critical comment on performance with the idea of being able to improve it.
5. *The learning gap*: usually called the 'transfer of learning' problem. The difficulty of translating knowledge and information into action 'doing'.

Topics for discussion

Complete your list of groups of which you are a member. When you have done this, compare and discuss these with anyone who also has an interest in group behaviour.

Reading list

Most books about groups are either psychological texts or handbooks for group leaders and groupworkers. However, the following are of interest:

Heap, K. (1985). *The Practice of Social Work with Groups: A Systematic Approach*. George Allen and Unwin: London. This book devotes its first seventeen pages to group membership in daily life and to some of the ways in which groups can help.

Milson, F. (1973). *An Introduction to Groupwork Skill*. Routledge and Kegan Paul: London. This is a very direct and simple text, which again starts from groups for everybody and then goes on to look at what happens in groups. There is also a chapter on observation, a skill which will concern us later.

2 Groups – what are they?

Some of the problems of studying human groups are:
- definition of the word 'group'
- group membership as common experience
- the problem of conformity
- the idea of condensation

What can be accepted as a 'group'?

Some of the most common categories of groups are:
- natural/artificial
- spontaneous/created
- large/small
- open/closed
- weak/strong

Dissimulation and expectation

Groups as systems of resources

Some of the factors creating interest in groups are:
- change
- social isolation
- answering the questions

Problems in the study of groups

This chapter explores the meaning of the term 'group' as used by various people and shows how the growing interest in groups, in particular 'artificial' groups (i.e. groups created for some specific purpose), has developed. It covers definitions, conformity, weak and strong groups, expectations, groups as systems of resources, change and social isolation, and tries to answer the question in the title of this chapter.

One of the primary problems in the study of human groups is that the term 'group' is commonly used to cover a multitude of gatherings both live and inanimate. What follows is that everyone believes that they know with some certainty what is meant by the word 'group' whenever it is used, even though the context in which it is used, as in the study of group behaviour, may be new and different.

A second related problem is concerned not so much with the term 'group', but with the common experience of being a member of one. In this case, the problem resides in the fact that because group experience is life-long and thus extremely common, it is taken for granted; unless, of course, special circumstances arise which cause an individual to become concerned with the effects membership or non-membership of a particular group may have.

When we start seriously to consider what a group may be, then we are compelled to make some points which can be used as the basis of our definition. Although human beings are almost continually in contact with one another, and although the members of a group are in contact with one another, this alone will not suffice as a working definition. If we look at the other end of the spectrum, we find 'isolation'. We tend to regard isolation – that is, separation from other human beings – as either an incredibly severe form of punishment (e.g. solitary confinement) or as total rejection. However, there are those who seek isolation, but unless this isolation is temporary in nature or the person seeking it is a mystic, then it is often felt that such pursuit is an irrational withdrawal from social life.

What is a group?

What then is a group? We have established that being a member of a group means being with others and that if one prefers isolation, one cannot be a part of a group – at least not at the same time. A simple starting point is time. If one could watch humanity going about its everyday existence, it would be like watching billions of small dots moving in small circumscribed areas. On this global view of humanity, we would see that most of these dots would, for both short and long periods of time, cease to move and would gather together with other dots before breaking away and clustering with a different set of dots. Some of these clusters would occur frequently, some only once; some would be permanent and others would be purely transient. Such clusters would be termed 'groups'. Thus the first really significant facts about groups are that they are composed of human beings, who remain in close physical proximity with each other for long or short periods of time.

But why do these clusters occur? There are several main reasons, the first of which is simple coincidence, of which people going to work form a good example. In order to get to work, many people have to gather together for a period of time (e.g. in a bus, train, tube, etc.). Their prime reason for doing so is to get to their place of work in the most convenient way. But in the process of achieving this goal, they are for a time aware that they are in the presence and company of others. Indeed, many commuters travel with the same people every day and an element of conscious choice often enters into the groups which form. The original accidental proximity is no longer wholly accidental and becomes a stage towards the second major cause of the creation of groups – choice or design.

Designed groups occur when individuals realize that in order to gain some fairly well-defined end, it is absolutely essential that they have the help of others. Such groups may exist for only as long as it takes to achieve the specific goal for which they were created. Others, where the reason for their existence is ongoing, or where the members find a strong satisfaction in their membership, may exist for much longer periods of time.

It is clear from the foregoing that all collections of individuals who are aware of each others' presence can be called a group. But it should also be clear that some form of dependence, as well as an increased awareness of presence, becomes the changeover point between groups which are transient collections and smaller and less transient groupings. Included in this category are groups as diverse as families, work-groups, teams, friendship groups, treatment groups and many others, all with interesting variations but all having members more or less dependent on each other and staying together for long periods of time.

When we start to look more closely at the groups of which we are members and at others which we may be about to join, it is essential that we recognize the degree to which these basic qualities exist. Put simply, such recognition is the first stage in the beginning of understanding of what goes on within a group and thus how best to use what it has to offer and what it will possibly demand of its members in return.

Because groups are formed for a variety of reasons, they tend to be given many different names and are placed in categories which serve to define purpose. This is essentially an exercise in distinguishing between different forms of the same thing and probably has as its purpose the enhancement of clarity. But there is a great deal of truth in the common belief that if you give something a name then two things automatically follow: first, that the differences between what is named and all other similar things become more apparent than the similarities between them; and, second, there is a sense that because something is given a name, it is not only distinct and separate but also knowledge has been gained about it.

These differences have been so elaborated upon in the literature on groups, group behaviour and groupwork, that anyone seeking information on groups is faced with a bewildering array of terms which seem to imply that the particular groups being written about are not just forms of a simple kind of human activity, but are essentially different animals. It is essential, therefore, not to go too far in accepting differences between groups and to remember that whatever is claimed as special for any particular group, it remains a collection of human beings aware of each others' presence and who have some need, however tenuous, of each other.

In order to clarify this point and make it possible for the reader to use these classifications of differences in the way that they were originally intended to be used (i.e. for clarifying the ways in which groups are used), I present briefly some of the more common and useful classificatory forms.

Classification of groups

Most classifications of groups are based upon accepting some principal characteristic of a group as defining it in distinction to other groups. Sometimes,

Table 1 Classification of groups by various criteria

Criteria	Classification	Characteristics
1. Nature	Natural/artificial	Familiarity and tradition/novelty and suspicion
2. Origin	Created/spontaneous	Conscious intent/generation by pressure of circumstances
3. Leader	Directive/non-directive	Different ideas of the basis of enduring change in human beings
4. Location	Environmental influences	The ethos, structure and management of the organization in which a group is embedded (e.g. hospital, school, etc.)
5. Members	Selection criteria	Principal characteristics of group members (e.g. age, gender, race, problem, availability)
6. Outcome	Group purpose	What the group is set up or adapted to achieve (e.g. learning, support, change, etc.)
7. Number	Size	The effects of large/small groups
8. Throughput	Open/closed	Whether group membership remains the same throughout the life of the group or not
9. Orientation	Approach	The selected theoretical base of the organization/leader/writer
10. Programme	Choice of activity	The principal activity used in the group (e.g. talk, drama, work, discussion, mixed, etc.)
11. Duration	Time factor	The length of group sessions or the length of time the group exists

Note: Items 1, 2, 7 and 8 are dealt with at some length in the pages that follow.

several principal characteristics are selected for this purpose in order to be more precise and more informative. The choice of such characteristics usually depends upon what is thought to be important to those who create, adapt or observe the group. Thus therapists will tend to define their group by the kind of human problems which are common to all the participants in the group. Alternatively, it might be defined on the basis of some particular theoretical orientation (see Table 1).

Depending upon one's viewpoint, any group can thus be classified in a number of ways and nearly all groups will attract several categorizations at the same time. Indeed, some groups start life as closed, leader-directed groups, but in the course of time become open and self-directed. But it should be remembered that all defining factors of a group are interrelated, which means that changes to one principal characteristic will have some effect on the others without exception. Thus it is not possible to increase the number of participants in an ongoing group without changing its methods of working, its interaction patterns and so on. Of course, groups may adapt to change and gradually assume a pattern of behaviour which is *similar* to that which was in operation before the change.

Finally, Table 1 provides details of some of the classifications in general use. It is important to note these details, because in the literature on groups they can often serve to indicate quite clearly a bias and a selectivity in the writer which may otherwise be overlooked to the detriment of being able to place such writing in its proper context.

Let us now look briefly at a few of the important defining characteristics of groups.

Natural/artificial groups

When talking about groups, most people accept that some groups are 'natural' and others are 'artificial'. This categorization, while almost universally accepted, has to be treated with care, because it often draws the distinction between those which are accepted and those who are rejected. 'Natural' has the connotation that it arises by ordinary processes, in the way that plants and animals came into being. However, this is not strictly true; the classification natural/artificial indicates not an absolute difference but a continuum. Groups labelled 'natural' are those which are part of the social structure of society. Thus the family, the prototype of all groups, is a 'natural' group, and so are all those groups which have arisen to facilitate human existence and which have a long history. Thus all human activities which are better or even wholly performed by individuals acting together tend to be labelled 'natural'. The fact that at some stage in the distant past such groups may have been deliberately created in order to ensure human survival or achieve other ends is of no real consequence. It is only the fact that they have become an integral part of social structure and have been so for centuries that earns them the descriptive label 'natural'.

'Artificial' groups, on the other hand, though created for exactly the same reasons as originally obtained for 'natural' groups, are often not crucial to the social structure, are of 'recent' development and thus without tradition, and are also not usually part of the everyday experience of members of society. So they are 'artificial'. This term is laden with suspicion, mainly to do with the purpose of such groups and also the intentions of their creators.

It is common for students of group dynamics, for instance, to investigate the processes of the study-groups of which they themselves are members. This is simply a means of using a group which has a somewhat 'natural' reason for its existence (i.e. as a seminar or tutorial group) as a subject of study. But upon suggesting that such a study should take place, those involved remark that the situation is 'artificial' (i.e. it is not 'real'). What they are actually saying is that the situation is one with which they are unfamiliar. It does not fall within the average person's experience of life to apply a conscious and structured examination to a group of people who are gathered together for what is usually regarded as a legitimate and 'natural' group process.

So the classification natural/artificial has a great deal to do with familiarity/ unfamiliarity and with the degree of conscious analysis which is applied to a group and is, in that sense, somewhat misleading. Indeed, even with the development this century of the processes of the analysis of behaviour, it is still common for the conscious analysis of human behaviour (except in moral or outcome terms) to be regarded not only with suspicion and some anxiety, but as something 'artificial' in the sense of not being natural or normal. But because we are now more concerned with the factors that might improve the quality of life and the performance of social roles, the deliberate examination of behaviour has become much more widespread and thus somewhat more 'natural'. Indeed, the whole purpose of a book like this is to allow enquiry into the function and performance of those groups in which we spend so much of our conscious time and to help us to begin to understand how such human resource systems work. The sense of observing and of attempting to understand a system of which we are a part without losing our place within that system or becoming separate from it, is to say the least strange, especially in the early stages of developing the relevant abilities!

Spontaneous/created groups

The difference between spontaneously occurring groups and those which are created is similar in kind to the natural/artificial distinction. Briefly, spontaneous groups form in response to the needs of a particular group of people at a particular time, who are in close proximity to one another. The factors involved are the immediacy of the problem(s) and the immediacy of the response.

Large/small groups

This is a very simple classification and is self-explanatory. However, it is instructive to note the general effects of size listed in Table 2.

Open/closed groups

In some ways, this is a very simple distinction to make, and yet in others hardly a distinction at all. The term 'open' is used in practice to describe a group (e.g. a club) where new members are enrolled and others leave. Therefore, although the number of members may remain the same throughout the life of the group, the individuals comprising the membership change (see Fig. 1a).

Table 2   The effects of size

Factors related to an increase in numbers in the group
1. Members become less satisfied with the group
2. An increase in the number of possible relationships
3. Any leader is required to become a more effective coordinator
4. Less time for each member to communicate
5. Most members tend to feel frustrated or threatened
6. The gap between frequent participators and others becomes proportionally larger
7. The resources of the group increase, so that it may be more efficient up to the point of diminishing returns
8. A reduction in the time it takes the group to do things but often accompanied by lower member efficiency
9. An increase in the number of ideas but more difficulty getting agreement
10. Problems of communication

Factors related to small groups
1. Less need for a leader
2. A belief by group members that they are less competent and that they possess less resources
3. Fewer ideas are produced and there is less indication of changes of attitude or in response patterns in general
4. Less coordinating behaviour by leaders and fewer attempts to clarify or to delegate authority
5. A much greater perception on the part of members that their group is successful in attaining group goals

The founder-members at point A in Fig. 1(a) are a, b, c, d and e. At point A1, the membership comprises a, b, c, d, e, f, g, h and l; at point A2, the members are d, f, h, k, l, m and n. Finally, at point B, when the group folds, only h and m are members.

On the other hand, a closed group is represented in Fig. 1(b). Here, all of the members started the group together and finished the group together. Although member e had a period of absence, no new member was recruited to take his place.

Exercise

Go back to the exercise in Chapter 1 (p. 6) and try to classify the groups you listed. Can you see how the characteristics of your groups can be classified? Does it start to explain why they were constructed or arose in the form they did? Does it help to understand why they were run as they were? For example, why do you think that most clubs are open groups with a large membership?

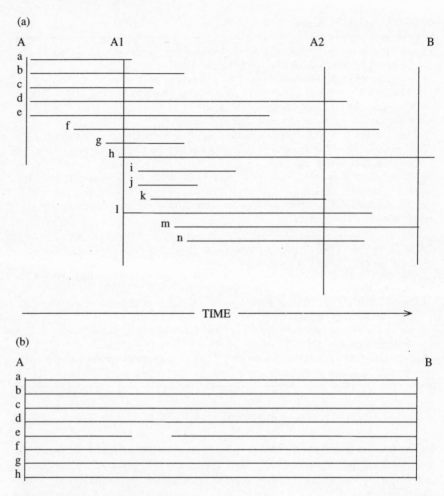

Figure 1   Open (a) and closed (b) groups.

Weak and strong groups (loose or tight membership)

As we have seen, the term 'group' is used very loosely. Some 'groups' have a very weak case for being called a separate entity, whereas others show much more evidence of their 'separateness'. Let us take an outrageous example of the former.

Having red hair may be a sufficient distinction to place one in a statistical group – that is, all those people who have red hair. If redheads were more susceptible to a life-threatening disease than non-redheads, then it would be a particularly significant group to belong to. But as this is not true, then the information does not help redheads to feel that they are a closely knit, inter-dependent group with some very distinct advantages to be gained from being in close personal contact with one another. This is a prime example of what can be called a 'weak' group; that is, the bonds between its members are virtually non-existent and as a group it tends to be recognized by people who do not belong to it. Also, as in this case, its sole reason for existence may be a vaguely statistical one.

> Weak groups are often statistical in nature and their members often have no close personal contact with each other or are even aware that they have been classified in this way.

If instead of red hair we had chosen cystic fibrosis as the element which identified a group of people, then the pointer starts to swing away from the designation 'weak' in the direction of 'strong' as a major characteristic of the group. Those who suffer from this disease are aware of others like themselves and are also aware that they can gain advantage by banding together, pooling their resources and information, and endeavouring to improve understanding of their particular problems among the general public. So they may well form an association which serves the purpose of uniting small local groups into a large national body with much more power.

The interesting thing is that although most members of such a national body choose to be members, the larger body they form is still a relatively 'weak' group because of its size. The small local groups, on the other hand, are much stronger groups and it is their power which supplies the drive for the larger group. So a strong group as defined here must be a group in which all the members know one another, meet frequently, have a serious commitment to the group and gain in various ways by their membership.

> A strong group is one in which the members are in close contact with each other, invest considerable energy in the group and gain from their membership in various ways.

This all seems very simple, though as one might expect, in real life things are not quite so straightforward, at least not very often. For instance, a group may be defined as weak even though its members are in close contact with one other. This may occur when the members are being held together by an external force and they have no real desire to be members of such a group. Such circumstances arise when individuals are confined to a building, perhaps because of their job. Thus it will become necessary, given the conditions that some groups work under, to explore how people who have no great liking for one another and consequently no great desire for closeness, can actually work together in a harmonious way.

Two factors are important if individuals in such situations are to function reasonably effectively: (1) each individual should be capable of gaining the respect of others in terms of his or her job competence, and (2) the organizational structure should be designed to accommodate efficient operators. These two factors are important for those working in care situations, as those being confined (i.e. the patients) do not always want to be there.

There are complications, in that strong groups can become weak and weak ones strong. Sometimes this may occur several times during the lifetime of a group. Nonetheless, the recognition that a group one is about to join or one is already a member of possesses strong or weak characteristics will affect one's expectations of it and of the demands it may make.

Dissimulation and expectation

Our expectations of what a group will be like are very powerful forces. I have seen many groups spend a considerable amount of time and effort developing high levels of trust and bonding to perform a function which could have been equally well achieved by a group with a disciplined structure and which was not dependent upon close personal relationships. But close personal relationships is what group members expect to develop in their groups and that is what they did.

Some groups offer a false face, pretending to be strong when in fact they are not. This *dissimulation* may emerge when members are encouraged to believe that they are there because they want to be, that great benefits will accrue. Yet the underlying level of performance is fuelled with suspicion, a lack of commitment, excessive caution and withdrawal. It is very difficult for a newcomer to the group to spot such a facade, and it may take some time to discover that what holds the group together are things like tradition, fear or even a lack of any visible or viable alternative.

Example

The leader of a home for single homeless men was an extremely powerful and charismatic figure. His staff were very loyal and were able to relate to him in a personal way. Thus the organization ran very smoothly and effectively with a great deal of caring and good work. But the organizational structure of the home was based wholly upon everyone liking the leader and through him relating to the other staff members. When, through a change in personal circumstances, the leader left his post, the organization fell apart. This apparently strong effective staff group had no sustainable structure. What had to be created was an organizational structure which reduced the excessive dependence on relationships of the previous group, and in which every member of staff knew where they fitted in relation to everyone else.

The lesson here is that the organization of a group should not be made on the basis that a particular group form – weak or strong – is always best, but that strong and weak forms should provide a balance appropriate to the needs of the situation at any particular time. When we come to discuss survival in groups, the ability to assess whether a group is operating in a weak or a strong way and also to judge whether what the group is doing is appropriate to its task, will be seen to be crucial in beginning to understand not only how a group is functioning but in finding one's place in it.

In the second half of the twentieth century, an interest has developed in the way groups work and how they can be used. Something which may have encouraged this interest is the increase in the size of organizations. This in turn has highlighted the stress factors which arise in such situations and has related them to the functional efficiency of systems. For instance, in an organization which is made up almost entirely of employees providing a service, it is not possible to think of such a system as being made up of anonymous individuals who have clearly defined roles and operate like cogs in a machine. As we will be constantly reminded, human beings are always aware of others when they are present. They always interact with, and form opinions about, these others, and like or dislike or ignore them. Such interactions can have significant effects – both good and bad – on the overall efficiency of an organization and must therefore be a serious consideration in its design.

If we look at the recognition of worth, the involvement in consultation of planned change or the lack of these things, we realize that the level of commitment proffered by individuals to achieving the aims of an organization may depend very much upon them. Workers in an organization respond very closely to how they feel their organization values their efforts and in particular how much they know they are able to influence decisions which may have a drastic effect on their lives.

Example

In a residential environment which had been created to deal with grossly disturbed children, the staff who had begun with great enthusiasm in custom-built premises and with freedom to develop their own techniques, gradually became less eager. Management decided that this was due to the novelty wearing off. But the decline was too steep and too prolonged for that to be the only reason. An investigation into the decline in performance standards came to no real conclusions and indeed appeared to have the effect of increasing the rate of deterioration. After several of the original staff had left, it emerged from their replacements that the stress in the work environment had no formally accepted place for its discharge. No support system existed. As a consequence, in order to diminish the stress related to their work, the staff began systematically reducing their contacts with their residents by making formal rules about availability, by setting up an appointment system and by taking long periods of absence from the unit. They also began to reduce their commitments in other ways, largely by substituting satisfactions which they now obtained outside of the unit for those which they had originally obtained within it. Some recognition of the value of these enthusiastic staff and some provision of a support system would have reduced the costs, exposed the problems and ultimately have saved the unit from massive deterioration in its standards of care.

Let us now look at some of the other reasons why interest in groups has grown so much. These reasons will, I hope, explain why so many more people are finding that their job includes some expectation that they can work in groups and that they should know something about them.

One important reason lies in the fact that human beings develop in groups (e.g. a family). If groups have such formative abilities, then it should not be too difficult to see groups specifically created as helping human beings to improve, learn or change. Thus the investigation of what made 'natural' groups work began, and the learning from these investigations began to be used and deliberately applied to defined situations and problems.

The group as a system of resources

Interest in groups has increased as the idea that groups can be created and their properties used to deal with a wide variety of human situations and problems has become widespread. Groups appear as a natural course of events, usually in order to perform functions which individuals are able to achieve with difficulty or not at all. What has changed, and in so doing has generated an enormous interest in groups, is (1) the spread of 'created' groups to many areas of human experience and (2) traditional human groups like the family have been subjected to scrutiny and analysis.

From these approaches has come a greater understanding of what kind of behaviour was produced when people gathered together for long or short periods of time. Artificially created groups arose designed using the knowledge of what happened in natural or spontaneously occurring groups. This was achieved by selecting certain of the patterns of natural groups and applying them to defined situations and problems. Unfortunately, this simple procedure produced so many different approaches that the simplicity and logic became submerged in a maze of theoretical ideas. Once these approaches were formulated, they each fought hard for recognition and in so doing over-emphasized their separate and individually different natures.

But behind this mass of approaches and theories lies the very simple fact that human beings are social animals. Being a member of many groups is essential for our very existence. All that any artificially created groups can hope to achieve is to isolate and recreate certain aspects of our naturally acquired group membership behaviour.

If something bulky and heavy has to be moved in the absence of suitable machinery, then several individuals operating together are more likely to be effective than one individual alone. Thus one of the basic resources of a group is the simple fact of number.

As we have seen, weak groups are those in which people tend to find themselves as a result of involvement with something else (e.g. a job). There are work situations in which a number of workers are in close physical proximity to one another in a building, but who could probably perform their tasks just as well if they were isolated from each other. The fact of their being together stems from other considerations than any value deriving from being in a group. The organizational structure in which such people work is what holds them physically close together, not any great need to be in a group. Number is not really a group asset in this case. Such a group might work more efficiently if its members took advantage of their being physically close; however, the increased socializing could operate as a counter to whatever increased communication took place.

But number does produce one inalienable asset for any group because there is an accumulation of assets and resources. Sometimes, as in weak groups, these assets and resources can be used as individual resources – for example, the individual skills of members of a typing pool – without the need to pay too much attention to the fact that each individual works in close proximity to others. While one can easily recognize human resources like secretarial skills, it is not so easy recognizing other very important resources like experience, knowledge, understanding, support, compassion, etc. Yet it is just such human resources which have received so much interest and attention lately. Why? Well the argument goes something like this . . .

Human beings are raised in groups, which, even if they comprise only one parent and a child, are themselves part of a larger group, such as an extended family or a small community. So whatever kind of person emerges from the growing-up situation, group influences have played a major part in that development and will continue to do so. Thus if a person experiences problems in life which derive from the kind of person he or she is and it becomes necessary or expedient to support or change that person, then, it is argued, it would be logical to use similar processes to those that formed the person in the first place (i.e. groups) to effect the change.

Such cooperation is used not only to perform a simple task, which when finished will leave the participants relatively unchanged, except perhaps for increased levels of satisfaction and familiarity with the others involved; it is cooperation designed to bring about change. Even more important, the change is to be directed at the members of the group through the processes of sharing, learning, giving and receiving information, being exposed to different ways of thinking and doing.

The concept of change being brought about in a group situation is not new, but the emphasis placed upon it in our society is. We do not have to look far for the reasons for this. Stress has increased enormously in our society, along with the need for flexibility and the need to adapt to rapidly changing conditions. Many people are ill-prepared by their upbringing to cope with this kind of situation.

Another factor has been the increase in the likelihood of *social isolation*. Mobility and the need to move away from home in order to obtain work are the usual explanations offered here, but whatever the truth of these ideas the stability and security which once existed in static extended families, however stultifying it may have been, no longer exist. This is apparent when things go wrong and there are no immediate sources of help or information available, except that offered by professional helpers. Thus many people feel that not only do they have the responsibility to deal with their own problems themselves, but because they are poorly equipped to do so, they see themselves as 'different'. This is often translated into feelings of inadequacy and of isolation.

When a group of people with a common problem gather together, they soon discover that, despite the enormous differences which exist between them as individuals, others have the same or similar difficulties and face the same kinds of problems when attempting to cope with them. This is the first step in helping to diminish such feelings of isolation and difference.

Example

A group of single parents was formed by social workers after a great deal of hard work, which involved providing transport, a meal at each attendance and child-minding facilities. Initially, the members of the group were suspicious of each other, but as it became clear that they faced the same difficulties, they became freer in their conversation. The social workers, who were not new to groupwork, were surprised by the number of such statements as: 'Oh! I felt I was the only one who felt like that', or 'I am glad to hear that's what you do – I thought I was going barmy!'

When you know that others are acting, thinking and feeling about a problem which they have in common in roughly similar ways, because you can see and hear it happening, there is a powerful sense of relief which flows from that knowledge. It is even more powerful if the knowledge of similarity is acquired in a face-to-face situation, when it has the impact of direct personal understanding without the intervention of others. The individual's own senses have a higher degree of credibility than when information is conveyed by others.

We are now in a position to make some summarizing statements, which are in effect answers to the question in the title of this chapter. Thus, what is a group? A group is a collection of individuals who continue to meet with each other over a period of time and who develop a stable pattern of relationships which allows them to discover and use the potential and actual resources both collectively and individually which are thus made available.

Why so much interest? The answer to this question cannot be given with absolute certainty, but as I have suggested in this chapter it might consist of two major parts. Interest in groups has grown enormously in our society during the twentieth century because they may be used as replacement support systems for the extended family. Also, it has become necessary to understand how groups function because we have become very conscious of the effect that human relations (i.e. the awareness of the presence of others) has on the efficiency of organizations and systems.

Summary of main points

A group is a collection of human beings and the patterns formed by such collections are universal. For our purposes, it is necessary to be rather more specific than this, and therefore time spent together is used to distinguish between a group and a collection. Another helpful distinction is between 'natural' groups and those which are deemed 'artificial' – the latter are usually created deliberately. The final distinction we drew was between groups which are weak (i.e. where the bond between members are not very strong or important) and those which are strong.

List of basic concepts and terms

In this chapter, we have covered the following concepts: conformity; condensation; natural/artificial groups; difference; spontaneous/created groups; the size of groups; open/closed groups; weak/strong groups; expectations of members; stress; the group as a resource system; change; and isolates.

Topics for discussion

A group offers each of its members a number of potential relationships. Calculate the increase in the number of such relationships when the membership of a group increases from five to ten. Don't forget that relationships are not just those which are on a one-to-one basis; they are also found in sub-groups of three, four, five or more up to the total number in the group.

   Why do you think that people accept groups more readily when they think them to be 'natural' or 'spontaneous', rather than 'artificial' or 'created'?

Reading list

Aronson, E. (1980). *The Social Animal*, 3rd edn. W.H. Freeman: New York. Pages 13–50 cover the complex area of conformity, which is so basic to any understanding of how groups operate and of the pressures they can exert.

Douglas, T. (1993). *A Theory of Groupwork*. Macmillan: London. Chapter 4 is specifically about the resources of groups, but the whole book is concerned with the idea that working with groups is largely a matter of recognizing and using the resources which groups possess or can develop.

Hare, A.P. (1962). *Handbook of Small Group Research*. Free Press of Glencoe: New York. Pages 224–245 cover most aspects of group size and the effects that different sizes have on group performance.

3 Different ways of 'seeing' groups: explanations and theories

Introduction
The approaches: basic assumptions
Five approaches:
• Group dynamic
• Psychodynamic
• Behaviourist
• Systems
• Humanistic
What they have to offer the group member

Introduction

As we saw in Chapter 2, there has been a growth in the interest in groups and also in speculation about the ways in which individuals operate in them. In particular, as the realization has grown about the essentially social and group-oriented existence of human beings, more attempts have been made to discover the advantages and disadvantages of group systems.

Quite understandably, then, there have also developed a large number of explanations of group behaviour, some based in and derived from more general theories of behaviour, whereas others have drawn specifically on the direct analysis of existing and experimental groups. The profusion of such 'explanations' is confusing to those turning to the literature for help in understanding group situations in which they find themselves, either at work, at leisure or in the family. This chapter presents some of the more important theoretical ideas, important in terms of the value they may possess for those attempting to understand the complexities of group behaviour. Because these will be fairly simple statements of complex matters, frequent reference will be made to sources where more detailed material can be found.

It is not essential for a group member to adhere to any one of the approaches covered here, for none claims to cover everything, but some ideas will certainly be found to be more compatible with the individual reader than others and will thus probably be more suitable for that individual to use as a basis for his or her theoretical and personal understanding.

The essence of being in a group is that the individual, being a member, finds him or herself in the presence of certain others for long or short periods of time. If, as is usually the case, all the members are in each others' presence for the purpose of achieving something – even if it is just to avoid feeling lonely – then what is of paramount importance to those members and to the group is that they see and react to one another. It is scarcely credible that an individual can be in the presence of others without being aware of the fact. And being aware inevitably means that some response is evoked, even if it is only to ignore those others.

When people are asked to describe a situation in which they find themselves totally ignored, although surrounded by familiar people in well-known settings and unable to make contact at any level, they tend to imagine that they are either gravely ill or dead, or perhaps they have become some form of spirit. Such is our dependence upon being recognized by others, of being conscious of their response to us as a confirmation of our existence, that when we seek explanations of what goes on in groups we automatically search for material, theories and ideas about behaviour in the presence of others.

Before we look at some of these approaches, a word of warning is appropriate. Psychological and other theories about human behaviour are not collections, however elegant, of testable truths. Indeed, the very label 'approach' implies that they are rational and logical attempts towards offering an explanation of what for the most part is hidden, based on that part of behaviour which is actually visible and observable.

Thus our first task must be to show how and where these approaches start from; that is, to make clear the basic assumptions from which the theorists begin. If these facts can be made clear, then the value any such approach may have as an explanation of what we may find as members of groups will have been placed upon a much firmer footing. Above all, we may be less likely to accept one approach as being absolute truth and available for all our needs to know.

What we want from theoretical ideas about behaviour in groups are clues which will help us to understand what is actually happening in a group when we are involved in it. If this seems a very precise requirement, there are valid reasons for it. It is possible to become fascinated by ideas in themselves and thus to find that a whole new interest has opened up, but one which has little value for any on-the-spot understanding of group behaviour. Then there are those ideas which look good and useful when we are not actually in a group situation, but which need also to be equally good and useful when we are absorbed in the functions of the group.

So let us look at some of the basic assumptions which underlie the more common approaches and note how these assumptions dictate what is regarded as important and thus what forms the essentials of the theory. Then we will look at several different approaches and see what they have to offer as useful ways of 'seeing' groups. Finally, we will be able to draw some comparisons.

Basic assumptions

There are probably only four basic assumptions which need concern us here:

1. The degree to which it is considered we have the freedom to shape our own lives or, alternatively, the degree to which those lives are determined by factors over which we have no control.
2. The degree to which inherited (i.e. genetic) factors control our development and behaviour or, alternatively, the degree to which experience and learning play a part.
3. The sources of our motivations and the directions such urges to action take.
4. The closeness to, or distance from, animal behaviour the behaviour of human beings appears to be.

Let us illustrate how one approach to the understanding of behaviour, based on one or more of these assumptions, conditions what is accepted. If the assumption is deterministic (i.e. it is established by pre-existing factors), then all the evidence for current behaviour will be sought in the historical past. For instance, any individual in the present will be regarded by those who follow deterministic doctrines as producing behaviour which is almost inevitable, because he or she has been programmed during development and growth to respond in exactly that way. Of course, they can learn to modify that programming, but the determinist viewpoint reminds us that what and how that learning takes place, its quality and effectiveness, and the use which will be made of it, are also circumscribed by the historical programming process.

Others believe that this kind of determinist assumption produces far too rigid an approach, and while they accept that programming takes place, they also believe that it can be modified by deliberately setting out to learn and to integrate new and different behavioural patterns. Indeed, not only do such people believe that change, growth and development are limited by the capacity of the individual, they also assume that searching for historical programming in order to find reasons for current behaviour is rendered a useless operation by the lack of supporting factual evidence. In any case, they argue, whatever evidence is adduced will have been distorted by the passage of time and the fallibility of recall and memory. So they concentrate on current behaviour which they can see. This allows them to look for the practical evidence of what advantage or disadvantage, what costs and rewards are involved for the individuals who display such behaviour.

The theories that appear to offer something of interest regarding group behaviour and which we will consider here are: Group dynamics, psychodynamic theory, behaviourist theory, systems theory and humanist theory.

Group dynamics

The term 'group dynamics' is used very loosely in at least two particular ways. First, it is used to cover the general study of the behaviour of people in groups and more specifically to cover those theorists of group behaviour like Bonner (1959) who are pragmatists and base their theorizing on their observation and recording of what happens in groups. In this latter instance, the group – any group – is seen as the unit of investigation, and it is in this sense that I use the term here.

Group dynamic material is pragmatic; that is, its practitioners take what they see happening in groups and, without attempting to explain it, record it. Thus it is also observational and descriptive in nature. There are, of course, problems with this approach, however much its basis in common sense appears to be. For instance, all observers introduce an element of bias into their recordings of what they see, often based on what they expect to see and their own particular idiosyncrasies.

The final point about group dynamic material is that it is cumulative. Thus material has been and is being collected from the recorded observations of groups made in all kinds of different situations and collated into what have become by practice areas of major interest. Thus if we want to know how the members of a group are likely to respond if they are of different ages, we can look up the data that are available on such groups. Or if we want to know what the probability is of a group developing in a particular way in a finite amount of time, we can refer to the data on such groups.

Group dynamics is an analysed collection of information about how groups have been seen to behave in the past. It deals in probabilities, in that it cannot say a group will do this or that. But it is able to predict whether the probability of a group behaving in a particular way under certain circumstances is high or low. A major limitation with such probabilities is that all groups behave in basically the same sorts of ways, with a reasonably close identity of performance in whatever situation they occur. In simple terms, this means that we have to believe that all groups are more similar to each other than they are different. But as we know, these generalities are just that – generalities – excellent as guidelines. But they can be no more specific because of the wide diversity of human behaviour patterns when considered in detail and because also of the wide variety of human situations in which groups operate. (We will discuss the implications of group dynamics for members of groups and those working in group situations later in the chapter.)

Fundamentally, group dynamicists are not concerned with the historical past of the groups they observe, but only with their current behaviour and the ways in which they attempt to achieve their aims and goals. Interestingly, the analysis that they make of how a group progresses towards its goals was originally described in terms of 'forces', that it is factors which either help a group towards achieving what it set out to do or which impedes it. These factors tend to be categorized into three groups: the nature of the ways in which group members interact with each other; the forces which emerge from the relationship of the group to the larger organization of which it is part; and the psychological structure of the group.

Group dynamicists list among those forces operating to create the character of the interaction process, such factors as the level of participation of members, the degree of cohesiveness of the group, the values which the group holds, the kind and quality of group leadership and the nature of the group's internal structure.

The influence of these so-called forces is easy to see. For instance, whatever power a group has flows from the energy of its members, so almost without question the degree of participation of a group's members dictates how well it is able to work towards its goal. Again a group which is riven with dissension has to spend all its time trying to heal breaches and soothe its members, so little energy or time is available to do the work it was set up to do. Alternatively, if the cohesion of a group is too great, it may be too smug, thus preventing it from doing very much. This is why the right balance has to be struck for the job in hand and why group dynamicists talk about questions of degree.

The value system that a group adopts will set the standards of behaviour, which may be anything from near absolute freedom to almost total restriction, a very potent force in deciding how well the group will function. The quality of leadership acts are the most obvious of the forces working for the good or ill of the group, be they the acts of designated leaders or of members. Finally, the structure of the group, which covers such matters as permissiveness, freedom, communication between members and others, the group's competitiveness, etc., are all factors which influence the group's movement towards its goals.

The second area concerns the relationship a group has with the larger groups of which it is a part. These groups can be as large as society itself or as small as another part of the organization. The important fact is that the larger group influences the smaller group because ideas, orders, beliefs, instructions and programmes flow across group boundaries. Though they also flow in the opposite direction, the essential point is that influence and thus pressure to behave in various ways flows into and out of the group. In dynamic terms, 'forces' are at work which influence the group's capacity to do its job.

The third area of group dynamic ideas concerns those forces which derive from such factors as how much the group members like one another, the roles each is able to play, the rules of behaviour the group devises for itself and, above all, how much each member finds the group rewarding and thus how much of themselves they are prepared to commit to it.

All of this is very logical and is located not in the past development of the members, but in the evidence of their current behaviour. Its weakness as a tool for understanding what goes on in a group is that it concentrates almost exclusively on what are believed to be those 'forces' which promote or detract from movement towards achieving some purpose. The problem is that all groups tend to have many aims, not all of which are compatible with each other. Each and every member of a group may have several reasons for being there, only some of which may equate with what the group as a whole exists for. Nevertheless, as a way to begin to understand how groups operate, it has the merit of being simple, being based on observation, and it is therefore open to observation and not complicated by complex analyses of individual behaviour patterns.

Psychodynamic theory

Freud's contribution to the understanding of group behaviour was based upon two assumptions: (1) that group behaviour stemmed from the patterns of family life and from his concept of the origins of society, usually referred to as 'the primal horde'; and (2) that a group is centred around the emotional relationships of its members towards the leader, as siblings to a father figure. Thus the nature of the relationship of members to the leader is that of infant to parent, and that of members to each other is the relationship of siblings. Such relationships are held to be subject to all the problems which beset siblings, including competition for the leader's approval, rivalry and jealousy. A group is deemed to be cohesive when these conflict emotions have been dealt with by a process of redirecting them (displacement) onto the leader, thus allowing members to identify with one another and to operate in an atmosphere of brotherly and sisterly love.

Interesting as this formulation is, it concerns only biological groupings. Freud left his followers with the enormous task of how to define social groups. The original Freudian definition of groups presented a model of groups which were in essence collections of individuals. This was particularly so for the outcomes of groups which were always defined in terms of the effects on the individuals who composed them.

Eventually, other theorists realized that this form of definition was too limiting and began to define a group as an entity in its own right – something which, if not greater than the sum of its parts (i.e. its individual members), was at least different and productive of outcomes. They could see that a group created a communications system which did not necessarily have the group leader as its focal and monitoring point; that members had much to share with each other and to contribute to the group as a whole; that the group developed a structure, in fact several structures, of roles, of communication, of rules and norms; and that it could also be successful in improving member perception, in stimulating interaction and in reducing the needs for defences.

This led eventually to two strands in the perception of groups. The first, mainly traditional, considered that the group was a *context* in which the individual member was the most important functioning unit. The second developed the idea that each individual member eventually became a part of a new unit – the group – and that this unit became the *instrument* of the most important outcomes rather than the individual members.

But because they never lost their strong interest in the individual, even when adopting the group-as-instrument approach, analysts brought to their interpretation of group behaviour the other Freudian concepts which related to individual development and behaviour. Essentially, those found to be most applicable concerned the various concepts of anxiety and the defence mechanisms which were considered to be engaged by the individual to avoid being overwhelmed by anxieties.

Anxiety is real enough and individuals can respond with fear when they perceive that some situation is a valid threat to their existence or their well-being. But apart from 'real' anxiety, Freud also postulated two other forms, the neurotic and the moral. The former was held to occur when an individual began to fear that he or she could lose control of basic instincts and perform behaviours which would attract some form of punishment. The latter was defined as an anxiety generated by a fear of conscience, usually appearing as guilt but originally associated with punishment.

Each member of a group brings to that group the anxieties and levels of experience that they have developed over time. The group, any group, is just another social experience, and each individual will produce behaviour largely stimulated by what they perceive is happening in that group – through their anxiety patterns and through the ways they have available to cope with them.

Some of the ways of coping have been defined as defence mechanisms. Among the most important for an understanding of group behaviour, and bearing in mind that such mechanisms (1) are unconscious, (2) allow relief from tension, (3) reduce anxiety and (4) do not affect self-esteem because their operation is hidden, are the following:

Displacement occurs when feelings and/or actions are transferred from the original target to another object that arouses less anxiety. Displacement is commonly argued to be the fundamental driving force behind the process of scapegoating. Often, enough blame, bad behaviour and untenable thoughts are transferred in this way so that those doing the transferring feel cleansed in comparison with their target of displacement, or relieved of their tension, anger or frustration.

Similarly, *projection* is a transferring mechanism which causes the undesirable traits of an individual to be relocated by that individual to other people or agencies. When this procedure is complete, it becomes possible to condemn in others – the targets of the transfer – behaviour which could not be condemned by the original individual in him or herself because of the enormous anxiety it would engender.

In the defence of *compensation*, it is believed that an individual's poor performance in one area is balanced by achievement in another, thus restoring self-esteem. Mechanisms which appear quite frequently in group situations are *intellectualization* and *rationalization*. The former involves denying the existence of anxiety-arousing feelings by discussing them in a detached and distancing intellectual manner. The latter is a plausible gambit which offers explanations for behaviour which appear to be reasonable and which fit the facts but which are not the real anxiety-provoking reasons.

Regression occurs when an individual, faced with a stressful situation, reverts to a previously held safe and comfortable stage of development. This situation is often encountered when a group is about to take a step forward into an area which is new and relatively unexplored. Some members will actually delay the group's progression by moving backwards to previous positions, propelled by an anxiety brought about by the fear of the unknown.

All of these mechanisms, as defined by psychodynamic theorists, are elegant ways of explaining observed behaviour which are consonant with the basic Freudian concepts of personality development. They are interpretative in nature and relate to the individual as the central focus. Because the basic theory is individualistic and deterministic, it is believed that adult personalities are fixed according to the way in which the first five years of life have gone. Only a limited possibility exists of what can be acquired later in terms of learned behaviour and even that is dictated by the programmed ability to learn.

Behaviourist theory

Behaviourists reduce considerably the historical element of behaviour and place much greater emphasis upon learning and upon the effects of the environment. The basic postulates of this approach are as follows:

1. Both normal and abnormal behaviour patterns are learned, are predictable and are considered to be natural.
2. The environment has a considerable influence on the control of behaviour, and the specific conditions of this environmental control are identifiable and their effects can be modified with a subsequent change in the behaviours they control.
3. The overt behaviour of individuals and of social systems like groups and organizations is not only susceptible to rational explanation, but can also be predicted.
4. The use of concepts relating to internal pathology and disturbance is unnecessary – behaviour labelled in this way by some theorists can be satisfactorily explained in terms of the consequences it produces for the individual and for significant members of society. It is preferable to define such consequences in terms of learned behaviour which is inappropriate and maladaptive, or showing behavioural deficits (defined as adaptive response patterns which are missing), or in terms of the function of social conflict.

Behaviourists assert that there is a broad range of behaviour which is influenced by the consequences it produces. This reinforcement may either be negative, which tends to reduce the behaviour, or positive, which tends to increase the frequency of the response. Behaviour is thus seen as a consequence of the interaction between environmental conditions, which include feedback and the individual's learned modes of response.

For the behaviourists, then, a group is a social situation in which the interplay of the conditions existing within that group, as perceived by the individual and his or her learned patterns of responses, produces the behaviour which the individual manifests.

Systems theory

In systems theory, the group is seen as a 'system', which in essence is an organization that uses energy to transform materials into an end-product. A group is a social system, of which the main inputs are the resources and energies of its members. Thus the activities of the members and their actual achievements are the end-product and constitute rewards in themselves, thus becoming a source of energy which causes the group to continue without the need for extra inputs from outside the group. This is referred to as a source of energy renewal, and when the group is not providing such renewal it is then that either the group breaks up or extra energy needs to be found from another source. An open social group, however, does not usually run down, because it is able to bring in energy from outside of itself and survive. The sources of such energy are other institutions, other people and other environmental factors. No social group is ever defined as being self-sufficient or self-contained.

What systems theorists refer to as *throughput* – literally the process of using energy in the creation of an end-product – is, in group terms, the commitment of the group to the tasks they have set themselves. The *outputs*, are the achievements of the group in terms of learning, the solution of problems, etc.

The repetitive patterns which occur in groups are described by system theorists as the *cycles of events*, the main factor being the recycling of energy, deriving as we have seen from the satisfactions of the members with their achievements. Satisfied group members are quite prepared to reinvest energy in the group once more to produce greater satisfaction, even if this is of a different order.

The entropic process of systems theory states that all forms of organization move towards disorganization or death. However, social organizations like groups tend to increase their ability to survive by acquiring reserves of energy or new sources of energy, and thus become capable of an almost indefinite postponement of the entropic process. This is often done by expanding the system to include new resources, while still preserving as far as possible the essential character of the organization. Part of this process, which is known as *differentiation*, involves an elaboration of the role structure within the group and also a greater degree of specialization for those roles.

Finally, systems theorists postulate what they term *equifinality*, which means that the goals of social systems can be achieved from different starting points and by pursuing different paths, though as systems tend to regulate their rules of procedure, the available paths do tend to reduce in number.

Humanistic approaches

The approaches listed under this heading came into being because some psychologists and others realized that psychology was becoming more and more divorced from the study of real people. Humanistic psychologists therefore began to formulate theories which were practically oriented and based on experience. As a result, they have spawned therapies and helping processes designed to combat alienation.

Maslow, for instance, coined the term *self-actualization*, which basically means that human beings should attempt to realize all of their potential. He postulated a hierarchy of needs, which stated that until the more basic needs of humans are satisfied, the higher needs will remain unfulfilled. The basic needs are physiological in nature (e.g. hunger, warmth and security), whereas the higher ones are belonging and love, esteem and eventually self-actualization. Together with Lewin, and using certain Freudian concepts, Maslow created groups designed to develop self-actualizing tendencies, which developed into the Training Laboratories in Maine.

Another humanistic approach was developed by Carl Rogers, which is usually referred to as being client-centred. Rogers believed that basically people were alright as they were and that there was nothing extra that they needed in order to be whole. All that was required was for them to be helped to take the shutters down and the blinkers off and let the light shine in. This, he proclaimed, would develop the actualizing tendency, unconditional positive regard and produce the fully functioning personality.

Humanistic psychologists also sought material from existential philosophers, largely in the area of how people may gain access to themselves. But of equal importance was the idea that an increase in political awareness was necessary, because the existentialists believed that alienation was caused by societal factors rather than by personal ones.

Experimentation with hallucinogenic drugs was a chemical method of taking down the shutters and it also provided insights into unused and unknown powers of the human mind. The final components of this approach were derived from Eastern philosophies.

The concepts important to group members, other than as individuals attempting to understand themselves, relate to the fact that humanistic approaches use groups as mini societies, established with particular structures aimed at developing the actualizing processes. Thus what happens within the group is the basic content of the group task; history is really only important in the sense that it is the source of behavioural manifestations within the group; feedback from member to member is seen as the source of learning about oneself; and the generation of honesty and sincerity in one's relationships with others and with oneself.

What have these different ways of 'seeing' groups to offer the group member?

The major philosophical distinction between the approaches outlined here resides in the degree of freedom or lack of it which each approach holds to be available to human beings to make conscious choices. Psychodynamicists postulate that unconscious forces control us to a large extent, and thus the pattern of behaviour is set very early in life and is only marginally modifiable by any process of learning. What value such ideas have for members of groups lies in the patterns of possible explanations of individual behaviour in a social context.

Thus each individual group member is seen as bringing to the group an assortment of responses which were determined initially by the kind of personality each member developed as they grew to maturity. So the processes of domination and submission, of fantasy, of defence, of anxiety, and the means of dealing with them, are all programmed into each member. They may have learned that their in-built responses to perceived situations are not usually favourably received, and so they may also have learned that they can interpose a control between the impulse to respond and the actual behaviour it would promote. Nevertheless, the impulse occurs and sometimes shows in the discrepancy between the controlled behaviour and the only partially concealed desire.

If the primary objective of human beings is to relieve themselves of tensions which promote anxiety and psychic discomfort, then what psychodynamics theory has to offer the group member wanting to understand how groups operate, is a way of describing the possible behaviours and motivations of individuals who are seeking to adapt and utilize a social situation to meet their own specific security needs. In one sense, this tends to obviate any submission on the part of the individual to become a part of a greater whole. It would indicate that individual responses are selfish in the sense that integration with, and submission to, the group can only go so far as two factors will allow: first, the need to maintain personal security and, second, the perception of how far the group by its actions supplies the needs of the individual.

It is easy to understand that large element of anxiety and frustration which some group members experience when they realize that the group is no longer meeting either their security needs or satisfying their other requirements. This anxiety and frustration may increase if the group in question is one from which physical withdrawal is not possible.

As we have seen, the reduction of intolerable anxiety by some form of displacement, projection and/or fantasy is particularly noticeable and indeed freely available in a group by virtue of the close physical proximity of others and their emotional involvement in group activities. Shifting bad feelings and the blame for particular events onto others can certainly appear vindictive, unfair and unjust, particularly if it is regarded as conscious and deliberate behaviour. Often, the response of others assumes that is so. Thus one of the main contentions of psychoanalytic theory is exposed – that is, that human beings are not as rational nor as self-controlling as may have been thought, and in essence the world has accepted that we are far less free to make conscious choices than we might previously have assumed.

Aggressive behaviour is another case point. In the Freudian view, aggression is an integral part of the nature of human beings, and although we may conform to rules designed to curb aggressive behaviour, the basic urge remains. In groups, the attempts of individuals to master their aggressive impulses may lead to the creation of rules for confining the behaviour of others, which in Freudian terms amounts to an attempt to arrange to protect others from our own aggression rather than to protect ourselves from them.

The behaviourist approach is equally as deterministic as the psychoanalytic approach, but whereas the latter asserts that the biology of humans almost entirely determines their behaviour, the former insists that the major determining factor is the environment. Perhaps the main point of interest for group members is that a group, if it exists long enough with a fairly consistent membership, can become one of the major conditioning factors in the life of each individual member.

Pressures towards uniformity and conforming behaviour can become very important, particularly when the individual has a great need to be accepted as a member of a group or in some cases where there are no viable or visible alternatives. If the behaviour of an individual member brings kudos to the group as a whole, then that member's status in the group will increase. Conversely, where a member's behaviour brings censure and punishment on the group, then that member becomes a pariah and may even be expelled. In behavioural terms, a member who needs the group will tend to produce behaviour that the group finds acceptable. Then, because the individual feels acceptance, the behaviour will be reinforced and will increase in frequency, intensity and duration. Behaviour can also be reinforced by the process of avoidance, as when a member avoids producing behaviour which he knows will incur the displeasure of the group and may elicit punishment.

Another factor which behaviourists point out about groups refers to contagion. As we shall see later, this implies that members appear to 'catch' certain kinds of behaviour from one another, particularly when the behaviour is such that it gains approval from the group. This may not be a direct process, but one which develops through understanding by observing colleagues within the group. Such stimuli can affect individual members even when they are not reinforced in any way.

For behaviourists, then, a group is a specific and defined learning environment where pressures to produce certain kinds of behaviour acceptable to the majority operate. If a group is really of little concern to a particular member, then those pressures can only be minimal and consonant with that member's feelings that he or she is gaining by staying in the group. If leaving is a viable option, then if pressures increase beyond the cost a member is willing to pay, that member will undoubtedly quit.

Because systems theory was originally derived from the behaviour of physical and material conditions, it is basically concerned with the sources and use of energy. Thus when it is applied to groups composed of human beings who can consider what is happening to them and consciously choose what to do about things, the basic entropic process can be arrested in many ways by the production of new inputs of energy through a conscious effort of will. But some groups make good use of the energy available to them, whereas others do not. This distinction is important, for one of the main sources of renewed energy for a group derives from the satisfaction of its members, who are therefore quite prepared to invest more energy in ensuring that it continues and thus that they continue to derive rewards from it.

Leaders and other perceptive and concerned group members can often be seen investing a considerable amount of effort and energy in a group which is apparently stalled and unsuccessful. They know or feel that if the group becomes rewarding for its members, then energy will flow to enable it to continue and possibly to thrive.

Another essential point derived from this theory concerns the effect of the embedded nature of all groups. All systems, as organizations, are usually part of other systems which are larger and contain within themselves systems which are smaller. Energy flows across these boundaries and affects the capacity of the various systems to fulfil their tasks. In practical terms, this means that groups can only achieve what their containing and contained groups will allow. Second, it also means that if change from these limitations is essential, then a distinct process of attempting to shift the boundaries is necessary before the group can commence on its defined task. If change cannot be achieved, then the task may well be doomed from the start.

Of the five approaches we have studied here, only one – group dynamics – is almost wholly and specifically concerned with human groups. The others have produced material on group behaviour only as part of general theorizing about human behaviour, and in the process have given rise to groupwork practices based in that theory.

Group dynamics is thus not a theory of group behaviour so much as a collection of ordered data about groups, which can be used to create guidelines about the probable consequences of groups composed in various ways and subject to specific conditions. Like the behaviourist approach, its material is derived wholly from what can be seen to be happening in front of an observer. In very simple terms, what group dynamics has to offer is an extensive collection of data about what actually happens in groups. From these data, various principles are drawn on the basis of the fact that they seem to occur with regularity in all the data that are available. For the group member, the advantage of this is that there are guidelines, markers as to what might be expected to happen in any kind of group situation. However, the snag is that although all groups follow sufficiently similar patterns, the rule which chaos theorists expound, that significant differences in the starting point of a system can make enormous differences in its development, is particularly true about human groups.

Thus the data offered in group dynamics about the developmental sequence of groups, about the effects of size, the qualities of members and so on, while generally true can be changed quite dramatically by differences in the elements which go to make up any particular group. Thus although this seems to be the most practical approach to the understanding of groups and seems to offer the possibility of prediction, the first statement that all group dynamic texts have to make is that the performance of any group can be changed by changing just one element within it or that is related to it. In fact all the dynamic elements of a group are both interrelated and interdependent. Having given this caution, let us now look at some of the ways in which group dynamic ideas are of value to group members.

Having already mentioned group development, let us start at that point. As a group starts to form, particularly if it is a group of strangers, it appears to go through a series of stages, not necessarily in strict linear sequence, as it develops from a collection of individuals into a unity with a degree of recognizable cohesion and a set of operating rules and norms. It is inadvisable to state, as some researchers have done, that this is the way groups develop and the process is special to groups. A more accurate description is that given the kind of societies in which groups have been studied, the prevailing social habits of those societies emerge in the way strangers relate to one another in small face-to-face groups. The process is of itself not very interesting, but what emerges from it is. For example, until the members of a group have passed a certain amount of time in each other's presence and discovered what seems to be the level of the security in the group, then they will not commit a great deal of energy to the process for which the group was set up. This is even more noticeable if the level of interdependence which the group requires in order to function effectively is high. Energy which is being spent on maintaining personal security cannot be released until it is safe to do so. This simple observation not only suggests that groups will not work as units until such time as they have established safety, but also that if time is short work can be obtained from a group only if the required security is provided by the structure of the group, which in essence means rules and leadership ability, or if the group is aware that no great level of security is necessary.

One of the most obvious facts about groups is that they contain different numbers of members and the effects of size have been studied a great deal. What flows from differences in size can be stated quite simply and one or two facts will be offered here. Thus large groups have more resources but may have greater difficulty than smaller groups in gaining access to them; large groups offer places for members to hide, whereas smaller groups tend to expose their members and make them very visible; small groups do not have the same ability as large groups to divide into sub-groups; and so on.

There are an infinite number of explanations in the literature of how groups behave, most of which appear to be common sense. They cover all aspects of groups, including communication systems, leadership, power, rules, norms, cohesiveness, goals, values, structures, roles, why some groups gel and others don't, why groups break up, why some groups are successful and why others stagnate, what kinds of interaction are best suited for what tasks, and what can be expected of groups composed of members with certain kinds of backgrounds, needs or abilities. But what is quintessentially important about all this material is that it is about the behaviour of *groups* – that is, about functioning units – and not about the behaviour of individuals in a particular group situation.

Summary of main points

The five approaches presented here serve to highlight some of the different ways in which behaviour in groups can be 'seen'. These differences relate to:

1. The degree of freedom human beings have to make choices concerning their lives.
2. The degree to which various sources of influence are regarded as primary (e.g. genetic endowment, experience, the ability to learn, the environment).
3. The degree to which groups are envisaged as collections of individuals operating within the context of a specific social environment.
4. The degree to which groups can become social units in their own right, different to and in some senses superior to the sum of their individual members.

List of basic concepts and terms

Most of these are explained within the text and by the context in which they are used. The basic concepts are listed above.

Topics for discussion

1. What are the implications for understanding what goes on in a group starting from:
   (a) a psychodynamic perspective?
   (b) a group dynamic standpoint?
2. What do you understand by the term 'system' when used to describe a group?
3. From your own experience, consider the effects of:
   (a) anxiety about personal security in a group,
   (b) lack of commitment to the group programme,
   (c) being in a group from which one cannot leave when the group is either effective or ineffective.
4. How do you consider a group can affect the development of an individual as a positive self-regarding person?

Reading list

The literature on the approaches to groups is plentiful in terms of the way ideas are used in the practise of 'groupwork'; however, there is not much on the theoretical concepts and their applicability to the understanding of group behaviour.

Glassman, W.E. (1995). *Approaches to Psychology* (Second Edition). Open University Press: Buckingham. This is well-balanced general introduction to some of the major approaches. The author covers the biological, behaviourist, cognitive, psychoanalytic and humanist approaches.

Bonner, H. (1959). *Group Dynamics: Principles and Applications*. Ronald Press: New York. A very comprehensive text on the origins and growth of group dynamics, it contains a great deal of useful information for those interested both in the concept of generating theory from the process of accumulating and collating huge quantities of data, and in analysing it in terms of the probability of occurences.

Much has been written about the uses of systems theory in areas like social work, but one of the clearest and most succinct presentations of the main themes of open systems theory is to be found in: Katz, D. and Kahn, R.L. (1969). Common characteristics of open systems. In *Systems Thinking* (F.E. Emery, ed.). Penguin: Harmondsworth.

For the most important thinking on humanist ideas, see Maslow, A. (1968). *Toward a Psychology of Being*. Harper and Row: New York, which presents the concept of self-actualization and the hierarchy of needs. See also Rogers, C. (1973). *Encounter Groups*. Penguin: Harmondsworth. Technically, this slim book is a description of encounter groups which arose out of humanistic psychology. In the process of describing his work in this area, Rogers covers most of the approach's basic ideas.

4 What goes on in groups: a look at 'processes'

Introduction

In this chapter we examine what are known as 'processes' – that is, what are often referred to as the 'patterns' of group functioning which develop over a period of time. We look at some of them in detail and point to the main features by which they can be identified.

Once some of the processes which occur in all group situations have been described, we look at the ways in which these processes can be recognized in real-life situations. For while a theoretical knowledge of group processes may be very interesting, unless it is accompanied by an ability to recognize such processes and thus set up a range of choices of what one might do about them, in practical terms such knowledge is sterile.

Defining 'processes'

The *Collins Concise English Dictionary* (1988) defines a 'process' as: '1. a series of actions which produce a change or a development. 2. a method of doing or producing something. 3. progress or course of time'. Inevitably, we will find that group processes have something of all three definitions. Take the first process we are going to consider – interaction.

Interaction is a term used to describe the process which occurs between human beings who are in each other's presence. They react to that presence in a way which is based upon their perception of the situation and their past experience of similar situations. Thus psychologists tell us that an individual, merely by being in the presence of others, produces a reaction to his or her perception of that presence in terms of its apparent behaviour and appearance. Over a period of time, this action and reaction will occur many times and will produce consequences based on the cumulative experience. Perhaps some growth of understanding, perhaps the development of some friendliness and trust, or maybe their opposites dislike and mistrust, will occur. If we now analyse this paragraph, we will see that all the main elements of the dictionary definitions are there.

But there are several major processes which occur in groups, so how do we distinguish between them? The answer is in fact quite simple – the different processes are defined on the basis that they are actions which cluster firmly around a particular area of activity, for example the making of a decision. Of course, this defining could go on indefinitely, but in practice we restrict ourselves to those processes which appear to be most important to the life of groups.

The nine processes which we are going to look at are: interaction, communication, consequences, roles, decision-making, cohesion, the formulation of group aims, resources and change. It should be noted that while these factors are all processes, some are rather different in kind to others.

One further point. In the groupwork literature, there is frequent reference to 'group process', which often confuses readers. The distinction is, however, quite simple. 'Group process' in the singular defines the whole constellation of actions, reactions and behaviours which a group makes on its way to achieving its aims. In this sense, the processes we are about to consider are sub-processes.

This is probably the most important chapter in the book for those who work with people in groups, especially where they have some need to be able to influence the outcomes in selected directions. Being able to see and understand group processes is crucial to one's ability to work with people in groups, no matter how loosely such groups may be structured. Membership of a group always affects the way an individual behaves, although it is seldom very clear on a face-to-face basis that this is so.

The processes

Interaction

In Chapter 5, we suggest that groups are a form of social system. One of the prime factors in the definition of a system resides in the idea of elements which

Table 3 Where interaction arises and its effects

Interaction arises from:
1. An awareness of the close proximity of others
2. The establishment of lines of communication
3. Frequency of exposure of members to each other
4. The level of intensity of that exposure
5. The need to have approved behaviour reinforced
6. The capacity of members to be outgoing
7. The inclinations of members probably based on personality and past experience
8. Perceptions of similarity, liking, the needs of the situation, status
9. The need to access resources and gain insight and support

The effects of interaction:
1. It generates understanding
2. It spreads information
3. It enhances and confirms opinions
4. It facilitates group achievement

interact with each other. As we have seen, in a human group system, the elements are the individual people of which it is composed, and because they are thus in close physical proximity to each other they respond to each other's presence. In other words, they interact (see Table 3).

Communication

The process of interaction between group members involves some kind of verbal or gestural communication, and so we need to look at how communication works, what makes it effective or appropriate, and what factors block or impair it. Table 4 shows very briefly those situations which facilitate communication between members and those which restrict it, and there is some indication of what leads to poor communication.

One very important distinction in the communication pattern in groups which requires a special effort to understand when learning about what goes on in groups, is that which is made between *content* and *process*. For some reason, these two ideas about group functioning seem to be relatively hard to grasp, so perhaps it is advisable at this stage to spend some time trying to explain them.

The term 'content' is used to describe what people are saying in a group. This is simple enough, because it is something to which we pay attention most of our waking lives. We are often told, and indeed we act as if it were irrevocably true, that our society revolves around words; that indeed the ways in which we think are to some great extent limited and defined by the vocabulary we possess and can use. So far so good.

The content of our communication comprises the words we use.

Table 4 Communication

Communication takes place freely when members feel:
1. There is an atmosphere of acceptance in the group
2. There is evidence that real consideration is given to ideas
3. There is evidence that ridicule is not common

Communication is restricted when members:
1. Feel inadequate at expressing themselves
2. Assume that they will be ridiculed
3. Feel hostility towards other members
4. Feel left out of the decision-making process

Poor communication tends to arise when:
1. All comments are resented, even when valid
2. Members are so preoccupied with their own ideas that they do not listen to others
3. Members do not pay attention to what is going on
4. Most of the available time is hogged by individuals, thus reducing the participation of others
5. There is a refusal to spend time clarifying exactly what is under discussion
6. Individuals demonstrate their 'expertise' at great length
7. There is a strong tendency to introduce irrelevant material
8. There is an extravagant attention to unnecessary detail
9. Resolutions are made which block various kinds of contributions
10. There is a refusal to move from a subject area, although there is ample evidence that it is not relevant

---

When we come to consider 'process', we find ourselves in a much less readily understood area, for process is used to mean all the things which happen in communication between individuals, both in the short and long term, but not the actual words which individuals use to communicate with each other. Thus if a group member says, 'I am getting bored with this group. We are getting nowhere', the meaning of the words (context) is quite clear, at least at face value. The member is announcing that he or she is losing interest in the group because it seems to them that the group has lost its way. Most members of the group will interpret this statement in a fairly similar way. But what happens as a result of having heard and 'understood' the meaning of this statement is part of what the word 'process' is meant to describe. For instance, the members of the group may ignore the statement and continue with what they are doing, with the consequence that their acceptance of the member who made the statement may diminish markedly. On the other hand, they may be curious and somewhat surprised, it never having occurred to them that what they were doing could be described as 'boring'. They could be angry, resentful or any number of different responses could occur. But the one thing all these responses have in common is that they would produce consequences for the group which have very little direct connection with the words contained in the statement.

Process is what occurs as a result of some form of communication be-tween members of the group or other individuals.

If this explanation of 'content' and 'process' has actually meant anything, it should have served to indicate that although we are very familiar with the idea of paying attention to the meaning of words (as we believe them to be), we need to be equally aware of the processes which words can set in motion. And it is just this degree of sensitivity which is required by group members if they are to become aware of what effect communication is actually producing.

Let us for a moment just continue the story of the group member who said he was bored, and who is puzzled by the reactions of group members to his statement. After the group session has finished, he talks to one of the other members and thus begins to realize that his colleague was very hurt by his suggestion that he was bored, and as a result pointedly and deliberately excluded him in his mind from membership of the group. Of course, the 'bored' member will argue, quite honestly, that he had no wish to offend anyone, and that he was only stating how he felt – a matter which he thought would be of some interest to his colleagues. He will then possibly be forgiven, but it will be suggested that he could have phrased it differently, timed it better, etc.

Words, therefore, have meanings which in themselves are always understood in ways similar to the intentions of those who utter them by those to whom they are directed. But even when understood, the consequences in terms of what those words set in motion are infinitely more important for an understanding of what is going on. Indeed, those consequences sometimes have a habit of being very long-lasting. For instance, the bored member of the group we have just been considering may never be bored in that group again, but it is more than likely that his fellow members will continue to harbour some suspicions that he is bored for quite some time afterwards, they may make jokes about it and they may also develop other feelings shaped by this incident which will condition their future responses to him.

In seeing what is really going on in a group, it is necessary to pay a great deal of attention to process.

Indeed, in the early days of learning, it is necessary to pay more attention to process and consequence, thus balancing the excessive importance which we have already learned to attach to content and meaning.

Consequences

It is a truism that what we do not know about cannot be considered. Thus a considerable degree of understanding of what actually goes on in groups has to be derived from observation over time and, as always, from the codifying and organization of that experience.

> It is necessary to know (that is, to see) what is going on in a group if one is to have any chance of making a rational and conscious choice about how to behave within the group.

Observation is commonly related to the act of seeing, but in the context of groups it must also include reflection (i.e. thinking about what has been seen). It must also include what one has felt. This kind of observation requires a great deal of consideration, which we will go into later. Suffice it to say here that a number of our feelings are relatively 'untrustworthy', which is not to disparage them as feelings but to question their source and thus their relevance. They need to be assessed carefully for bias, both particular and personal, before they become reliable indicators of what we are actually experiencing. Once we have some idea of what bias exists, it can thereafter always be allowed for in our assessments of group situations.

What I would like to concentrate on here is the bedevilled question of inter-pretation. So let us make one thing absolutely clear from the beginning:

> All incoming sense information is interpreted.

When we come to observe human behaviour, interpretation tends to be mark-edly idiosyncratic, prejudiced, biased and derived from past experience. It could hardly be anything else. Thus when we find ourselves ascribing causes to ob-served behaviour (e.g. she did that *because* she was upset), although the ascrip-tion may be correct, it may also be either only partially correct or almost wholly wrong. It is not logically possible to be sure of the causes of observed effects, as a substantial amount of guesswork usually enters into the equation. Indeed, there is no way that all or even most of the actual causes of behaviour are available to an observer. They may not even be consciously available to the actor – that is, the person producing the behaviour. It is often stated that a person taking action in a situation usually explains his or her behaviour as a response to the situation as they saw it, whereas an observer has a strong tendency to describe the same behaviour as stemming from the personality of the individual taking the action.

But what is always available both to those who take action and those who observe it, are the consequences of that behaviour, both immediate and long term. But even here a degree of caution is necessary.

Consider the following:

A decides to go out.
A opens the door to the outside.
At that very moment it starts to rain.

Because one observable fact immediately precedes or follows another, there is often a sense that the one which occurred first actually precipitated the second. But it is clear that in A's action above, the sequence was purely a matter of coincidence. In this case, it is very easy to spot that fact. But in the complexities of group behaviour it is neither so easy to see coincidence for what it is nor to note when real consequence, cause and effect occur. Indeed, the real cause of a current situation may reside in the past and have but little basis in the group at all.

However, because many responses do occur in direct relationship to current behaviour, the observation of consequence is considerably more likely to be accurate and reliable than any attribution of cause.

> An understanding of what goes on in a group is more reliably formed from observation of the consequences which arise like ripples from particular incidents of behaviour than from any attempt to ascribe causes.

Roles

In all groups, the members play different parts more or less according to their perception of what is required and to their understanding of what they are able to do. In some groups and organizations, what role a person plays is determined by the organization in the light of what it deems expedient or necessary to fulfil its own purposes. But there is often a discrepancy between what a person performing a role believes they are doing and what those who observe the performance of that role believe they see happening (see above).

The following is an extract from an unpublished report I made on a hostel for homeless men some years ago:

> By creating a situation in which all people spoke to us with a reasonable degree of freedom, we were able to cross-relate all references to individual items of performance. In this referral system it became clear that people working together, believing implicitly that they were all pulling in the same direction, could often be shown to be pulling in different, sometimes opposed, directions and wasting scarce resources as well as drastically reducing the performance of the organization.

Example

Perhaps the clearest example of this was the way in which several staff members interpreted the role of a colleague compared with the way in which the senior probation liaison officer saw her own role. The officer was asked to define the important role she played and said:

(a) 'I see myself as being a support for the staff if they require assistance'.
(b) 'I introduce the monthly meetings'.
(c) 'I assist the staff in the selection of residents'.

Of these three perceptions of her role, only the last was seen as clearly by the other members of staff. No other staff member even thought the monthly meeting between the liaison officer and staff memorable enough to mention, and there were grave misgivings among the others about her support role.

I think the inferences here are very clear. If members of a work group think that they are performing their roles in the way they believe is expected of them, they will seldom feel any need to check that this is actually the case as far as their colleagues are concerned. The crucial result of this extremely common situation is that members of the work group become frustrated because they cannot understand the response their behaviour elicits from others. Because of this lack of consensus regarding their role and thus a lack of understanding of the 'real' causes of the behavioural response, a strong tendency develops to ascribe reasons which are usually related to the assumed personalities of those involved (see above).

All is not always as it seems, and this is a very good precept for all group and team members to bear in mind. Few groups contain all the factors which relate to the behaviour which emerges within them, for the simple reason that most group members spend infinitely less of their time in any one group than they do out of it. So this caution is a very apt counter to the facile assumption that behaviour which is observed within the group can be wholly explained in terms of the group's existence.

It is essential that all group members in all kinds of groups should understand and make some allowance for such differences in perception. Indeed, such differences when made visible can and often do form the basis of very positive group assets. Differences in perception can form the basis of new and previously unthought of approaches to problems and difficulties. Even more so, they form the basis of growing trust, because as they become apparent there is no further need to find reasons for behaviour which must, inevitably, be largely spurious.

Decision-making

In essence, making decisions in a group means choosing between situations which are known to be available. So the first factor to be borne in mind is that decisions are usually only as good as the information which was available at the time the decision was made. It is also necessary to bear in mind that sometimes active decisions are not made and as a result inertia and drift occur. But these are in a sense decisions – that is, decisions not to make decisions – and as such are quite often suitable and effective in particular circumstances. On the other

Table 5   Stages in the making of a decision

1. Recognize that (a) a problem exists and (b) that choices need to be made
2. Make as sure as possible that the nature of the problem or choice is clearly understood
3. Discover how many ways are available to deal with the problem or choice by gathering facts
4. Keep the group's discussion and thinking about the problem or choice relevant and to the point
5. Occasionally collect all the information and material together and summarize it so that all group members can see what is available
6. Attempt to analyse the major possible consequences of implementing any or all of the proposed solutions
7. Endeavour to establish the responsibility of the group and of individual members for the emerging decision and of their level of commitment to it
8. Make the choice or decision
9. Implement it
10. Evaluate it

hand, they may be symptomatic of a group unwilling or unable to work. As we shall see in Chapters 7 and 9, knowing the broad general processes of the decision-making process is part of a group member's survival equipment and also a very essential basis for being able to influence group progress and outcome.

Decisions which groups make that have emerged from a process in which all group members have been involved are extremely durable and hard to undo. One of the major contributing factors to an individual developing a sense of helplessness or powerlessness in any organization, is the realization that major decisions which may affect his or her life are being repeatedly made by others and he or she is not able to influence the making of these decisions in any way whatsoever.

Involvement in group decision-making processes is not only an essential part of a member's survival kit, but also part of the learning necessary to be a competent group member. Whatever resources a member may have or be able to develop can only be made accessible to the group if the members know how to gain access to them. A major element in this process is how members contribute to the stages of the decision-making process. Not only are they offering information, experience and understanding to the particular problem or choice under scrutiny, but they are also demonstrating to their fellow members something of their capacities and abilities which can then be stored in memory for future reference. In other words, the process of being involved begins to make visible what would not have been so otherwise (i.e. exactly what skills, knowledge, information, experience, etc., the group has at its disposal).

Cohesiveness

'Cohesion' and 'cohesiveness' are used by writers on group behaviour to cover a rather large group of processes. The *Collins Concise English Dictionary* (1988)

Table 6 Factors affecting the decision-making process

Factor	Outcome
1. The size of the group	More members and more resources, but possibly increased difficulty gaining access to them
2. The clarity of group purpose	If a group does not know clearly where it is going, then decisions about how to get there are not likely to be very effective
3. The standing of group members	Members of low standing within a group are not often able to influence decision-making, as their contributions – if made at all – tend to be disregarded
4. The stage a group has reached in its life-cycle	Where members are still virtual strangers to each other, cooperative decision-making is not very likely for personal security(risk)reasons
5. The nature of the group task	Many group tasks are simple and clear; others are complex and unclear. The nature of decision-making is related to this factor
6. The abilities of the members	Their experience and level of social functioning
7. The structure of the group	Essentially, whether the group organization allows members to contribute to the process or whether decision-making is limited to particular members
8. Pressure	Resulting from internal or external factors (e.g. the degree of urgency and level of risk involved)
9. Hidden agendas	The unknown aims and goals of members which may be different to, or even hostile to, the general aims of the group or particular areas of those aims – the absence of common aims
10. Resistance	This may develop from fear of consequence, disbelief in the validity of aims, timidity, previous experience, etc.
11. Divisibility of the task	Where a group's task cannot be split into parts to be dealt with by selected members of the group according to their abilities, expert opinion may be swamped by pressures and thus some opinions will never be expressed
12. Communication structure	Restrictive structures are often efficient when time is limited and the task simple; in complex tasks, restricted communication patterns often produce inefficient decision-making

Table 7 The factors which bind members to a group

1. Sharing experience in the group over time
2. Developing relationships
3. Pride in the group and satisfaction with membership
4. The development of a common language
5. A growing sense of obligation and of responsibility
6. Being in receipt of positive feedback from colleagues
7. Being physically close to others, which increases the frequency of interaction
8. The recognition of common interests and purpose
9. The response to skilled leadership
10. The absence of disruptive members and awkward situations
11. A perception that the group offers protection against threat from outside the group
12. The intimacy of groups of a small size
13. The existence of a good communication pattern
14. A perception that the group is effective – it works
15. Members attach considerable meaning to the group

defines the verb to 'cohere' as 'to hold or stick firmly together: to be connected logically or to be consistent'. In essence, then, cohesiveness is the act of holding together or the factors which bring about such a binding. When we look at what these factors are (Table 7), we see that they are many and various; however, what they have in common is that they all contribute to the sense members acquire, that their group is worthwhile, that it is attractive to them, it gives more than it demands, it generates a feeling of security in that its members feel as if they belong to it and are wholly accepted by it, and that it delivers satisfaction.

Despite the many sources of cohesiveness in a group, which may in themselves be difficult to isolate, when a group performs in a cohesive way, the fact is immediately recognizable both to its members and to observers of the group. Thus it is common to say that cohesiveness is '. . . the resultant of all the forces acting on the members to remain in or to leave the group' (Festinger 1950). Thus because cohesiveness is easily recognized but difficult to define, it tends to be described by the effects it produces (see Table 8):

> Relative to low-cohesive groups, high-cohesive groups engage in more social interaction, engage in more positive interactions, are more effective in achieving goals they set for themselves and have higher member satisfaction.

> (Shaw 1974)

Group aims

Groups tend to be systems which have an end-product, an aim, an outcome, a target or an achievement, or even several such goals. Several factors are involved in the development of a group's aims:

Table 8 The effects of binding members to a group

1. To facilitate the flow of information
2. To reduce anxiety
3. To facilitate change
4. To increase the likelihood of members being susceptible to the influence of their peers
5. To increase group pressure and thus ensure greater conformity
6. To exclude deviants
7. To allow greater freedom to initiate to high prestige members
8. To increase the acceptance of responsibility by all members
9. To generate mutual trust
10. To reduce absenteeism and withdrawal
11. To make the common goals most important
12. To make members willing to defend each other and the group against external attack
13. To engender an increased willingness to endure frustration to achieve the ends of the group

1. The aims of any organization within which the group operates.
2. The aims of the leaders/conveners of the group.
3. The aims and expectations of the group members.

In each case, these aims are not singular. For instance, it is possible that the leaders of a group may have:

• *Personal aims*: designed to meet their own needs.
• *Group aims*: ends which they want the group to achieve.
• *Aims for individual members*: specific ends which may or may not be part of their aims for the group as a whole.
• *Organizational aims*: ends dictated by the policy of their employing organization.

It must be clear by now that with the existence of so many aims among those most connected with the group, it becomes essential to establish some simple and stated aims with which all those involved can agree. However, it is always a distinct possibility that other aims – often unstated, sometimes unacknowledged – will still exist and will certainly continue to influence the level of commitment and participation available to the group. These are often referred to as 'hidden agendas', which may fluctuate according to individual perception of what demand the group is making at a particular time.

Example: I came to get away from work

In many of the groupwork training sessions I have held, it is not uncommon to find that some of the participants are there not because they want to be – in the sense that they have some inclination to learn about groups – but because they have been sent by a more senior colleague, probably on the basis that it may be of some value to have a member of his or her unit who it could be claimed has some knowledge of groupwork. Or, alternatively, an individual may have elected to attend the course as a means of escaping for a few days from the pressures of work.

There is no suggestion that such participants should in any way be regarded as defaulters. What is primarily at issue is that their aims in attending the group are significantly different from others. Once these aims are known to the group, then it becomes easier to accommodate them. But had they remained hidden, then their effects upon the group as a whole could have been quite serious.

Because the aims of these members of the group are so different from what might have been expected, they (although unknown to others) produce effects which are often highly visible, yet just because their source is not known they are often badly misinterpreted. However, it must not be supposed that other aims do not exist among other members of the group, especially in relation to their personal aims, not that these aims will continue to have the same form and intensity during the life of the group.

So part of the essential understanding of what goes on in any group must relate to the fact that members, leaders and interested parties are all attempting to achieve outcomes for themselves and for the group – and even for outsiders – which differ from the officially stated aims of the group. The spin-off here may well be in the level of commitment to those official aims being dependent upon the perception of each individual member of how such commitment will either facilitate or hinder the achievement of his or her own important personal outcomes in the group.

Discovering and developing group resources

Groups often command a larger fund of resources than do single individuals and thus have the potential to perform more difficult tasks. But their achievements may fail to equal their potential because members of groups are not sufficiently motivated to contribute their resources to the common cause, or because members' efforts are not well co-ordinated.

(Steiner 1974)

When an individual joins a group, he or she becomes a member – if he or she stays long enough – of what can be described as a 'mini world'. The rules of the group may be vastly different from the rules of society and from those of other groups, depending on the purpose of the group. Because the members of a group are in close physical proximity to each other, sometimes for quite long periods of time, their behaviour becomes, in psychological terms, very 'visible'.

Such a situation lends itself to members behaving in ways which, while appropriate to the group, might not be suitable for their everyday life. Thus when members feel comfortable with the behaviour patterns which the group seems to engender, they may find it possible to do things which they would not undertake outside the group: (a) because they had never thought of doing such things until the group offered them the possibility, and (b) if they had thought of doing them they would have been inhibited by their perception that such actions would be regarded as unacceptable by others around them.

It is this sense of difference – of being freed to do things, of being able to say and act – which releases into the group materials, knowledge, experience, feelings and resources which were previously not only unavailable but unknown.

Example

A number of social workers attended a day workshop to discuss an authority's proposal for implementing a new programme for care in the community. During the day, the large meeting was broken up into small groups with the express purpose of giving each participant space and time to put forward his or her own views, comments, criticisms and suggestions. Because these discussion groups were small in size, the members of each included people who did not know one another, as well as those who worked together. Again, because the groups were small, they quickly developed a more intimate and friendly atmosphere. Because what they were discussing was of some considerable importance to them all, various bits of information were released for the group's consideration which, under other circumstances (i.e. in the normal routine of the office) would not have occurred. Included in this information were the usual things of how unevenly information about the proposed programme had been diffused, of how impossible it was to understand how each individual was personally involved from the nature of the documents they had received, curiosity about who had been consulted on the proposals, and so on. But more importantly, a newcomer to the authority offered the information that her previous employer had actually gone through the process of implementing a similar plan some months before. It immediately emerged that this particular social worker already had experience of the difficulties and problems involved, and also of which solutions had worked and those which had not.

Consider what this meant and why such knowledge of what had happened previously had not been offered before this late stage.

Here was a resource – knowledge – which by force of circumstances became available and allowed costly mistakes – in terms of time, effort and commitment – to be avoided. The reason why this information had not been offered earlier was simply because the worker concerned had not found her feet, and did not want to expose herself to her new colleagues before she was able to predict their responses reasonably well and thus be fairly certain of the areas of safety. She was also uncertain of who to approach, even if she had thought that her past experience would be helpful.

> What a group has to offer is a situation in which the exposure of resources and their adaptation for use is made possible.

To begin to understand how this process functions is essential to a basic knowledge of group behaviour. The example just quoted has other information for us also. The word 'resource' is sometimes difficult to explain, as individuals are apt to consider that it refers to material things, finance, numbers of people, equipment, etc. But here a resource of some considerable value was the past experience of one individual. It was knowledge of how a similar situation had been dealt with, and of what had proved successful and what less so.

As we shall see later, the process of locating, exposing and using resources like this need not be dependent on what was almost a coincidence in our example, but can be designed into a group's behaviour.

Bringing about change

What was partially described in the example of the workshop in the previous sub-section was a concern with change. For instance, it was stated that because the rules in the small discussion group were significantly different to those which guided the daily routine of the social workers' lives, they promoted and found acceptable different behaviour patterns.

Organizations produce both formal and informal codes of conduct which arise in order to facilitate the function of the organization. For most purposes, such daily routines are adequate, but it is necessary to remember once more that boundaries (in this case the rules of acceptable behaviour) have two functions: they define what is to be left out as well what should be kept in. No-one has the foresight to predict what may happen and to prescribe rules to meet all possible eventualities, though indeed many have tried. So some degree of flexibility is often sought and key personnel within an organization are often allowed to change, amend and bend the rules in order to deal with new or different situations.

The problem with this form of flexibility is that it rests upon the need to recognize that a situation has arisen with which the standard procedures cannot cope effectively. This ability is not copiously available, as people are often blinkered in their thinking and unable to move away from the usual channels. Groups are thus often created to bring about changes in behaviour, insight and thinking. But how are they created?

By taking individuals away from the normal organizational units in which they function to new and different groupings with different rules and personnel, there is a chance that they will respond differently and with fresh ideas. The spin off from this is that the experience may etch into memory the fact that change is possible. There are other and sometimes better ways of doing things, more open ways of thinking and the possibility of greater understanding of oneself and of others.

If all the factors we have just discussed occur in groups, how is it possible for an understanding of complex group processes to be developed? The answer resides in three factors:

1. *Observation*: literally learning to watch what is happening before one's eyes.
2. *Experience*: not just having it but correlating it and using it.

3. *Recording*: some form of keeping hold of what has happened and in what kind of intensity and sequence.

As we shall see in Chapter 8, these three factors form the basis of any logical and coherent attempt at influencing the outcomes of a group or the ways in which the group pursues those outcomes.

Summary of main points

Group processes are patterns of behaviour which form in a group over a period of time and which are usually larger than the behaviour patterns of individual members. Thus patterns of interaction, of communication develop which are relatively unique to a particular group. These patterns are what give a group its identity. It is essential to recognize them to understand the ways in which a particular group works.

List of basic concepts and terms

Because of the particular structure of this chapter, the concepts and terms are already clearly defined and individually discussed in the text.

Topics for discussion

Define the principal differences between individual patterns of behaviour and the patterns of the group processes of any group with which you are familiar.

If you wanted to influence the process of this group, how would you set about doing it? Think in terms of influencing individual behaviour, but pay particular attention to any processes which you may just have defined.

Reading list

Many writers refer to group processes but they seldom specify with clarity that this is what they are doing. I attempted to do just that in *Group Processes in Social Work* (Chichester, John Wiley & Sons Ltd. 1979). This is a very detailed and elaborate study of group processes, but it also uses charts, definitions and diagrams to clarify a developing understanding of the processes and explain them as the working habits of a group.

Shaw, M.E. (1974). An Overview of Small Group Behavior. *University Programs Modular Studies*. General Learning Press: Morristown, NJ. This paper is a typical example of the group dynamics approach. Shaw collects from a vast number of sources information about the major aspects of group behaviour, collates them and produces factual information about the likelihood of events occurring in particular group situations.

Steiner, I.D. (1974). Task Performing Groups. *University Programs Modular Studies*. General Learning Press: Morristown, NJ. A similar collating study to Shaw but this one concentrates on the tasks which groups undertake. There is some excellent material on decision-making.

5 The influences at work in a group

Introduction

In this chapter, we look at those factors which influence a group as it works towards achieving its goals. But we start by examining the group as a small social system, affected by the expectations of its members and constrained by time, and show how it develops a system of rules, some of which are highly visible but some of which are only discernible by the individual member when he or she becomes involved with them. Finally, we look at some of the external influences on groups, bearing in mind that few if any groups are not part of larger systems.

Influence

There is a simple connection between how much a group means to an individual and the amount of influence which that group can exert. Thus where a group is defined as such merely because its members work or live in relatively close physical proximity to one another, and although each is dependent upon the work of others, those others could be replaced without loss of efficiency, then that group has limited ability to influence the behaviour of its members to any great extent.

Another way of putting this is in terms of need. For instance, if a group provides a great deal of support for its members in a difficult and exhausting task, then their loyalty to the group will be quite strong. Therefore, if the group should make demands on its members in terms, say, of finance, time or behaviour, these are quite willingly met. But should the group fail to supply adequate support (in the perception of its members that is) at any time, then the demands it makes on its members become increasingly burdensome and loyalty tends to disintegrate. The result is bickering, complaints, evasion and defiance – even departure from the group when this is possible. This also occurs when the majority of members find an alternative support system which appears to provide a similar or better service for less cost in terms of demands made. A situation then arises in which people may continue to work together, but the group bonding becomes less strong as each member has much less need of his or her colleagues. Support now comes from outside the confines of the working group. It is often the individual member's family which comes to play the part of the outside support system – a burden which many families, through lack of a true understanding of what is entailed, find extremely hard to sustain. If this support system fails, individual work-group members are thrust back onto their own resources, which often means that in order to cope they gradually have to withdraw their commitment to the work situation, thus reducing stress and conserving energy.

> The influence a group can exert on its members in the absence of acceptable alternatives is directly related to the need members have of the support which the group can supply.

There are always group situations in which some members are wholly satisfied with what they receive from group membership and equally content with the demands the group makes of them, whereas others are dissatisfied on both counts. In such cases, the ability of the group to exert its influence on the thinking and behaviour of its members is patchy and uneven in quality, which may lead to diminished performance, dissatisfaction, disillusionment and almost certainly to continuous demands for structural change. It becomes increasingly clear in such situations that bad feeling is engendered between those who are satisfied and those who are not, so that the group tends to spend an increasing amount of time examining and re-examining its own structure and procedures to the detriment of whatever purpose it was originally created to fulfil.

> A group that is absorbed in an examination of its own structures and
> procedures has a markedly diminished capacity to function effectively
> with regard to its original task.

It is for this reason that newly formed groups have little capacity to work as
cohesive units except under very exceptional circumstances – they are too busy
creating their own internal structure.

Let us now attempt once more to put this matter of group influence into an
acceptable context. When an individual joins a club for whatever benefits the
club can confer upon its members, it will almost certainly demand something in
return, including fees, conformity to a code of conduct, etc. In making these
demands, the club or organization is influencing the behaviour of its members
directly. Behind all these demands is a very clear indication that if they are not
met in an acceptable way, the member will be expelled or the new applicant for
membership rejected.

These influences are blatant and obvious and are therefore reasonably well
understood, but others are much more subtle and far less available for scrutiny.
It is these latter influences which are to be seen only in the effects they have on
members – in the way they think, in the confidence of their behaviour, in the
changes in their attitudes and beliefs. These effects occur over time and are best
revealed by sound observation, which can be used to compare what is current
with what has passed, not just in terms of fallible memory but by reference to
some record, however slight.

> Change in a group or change in an individual's perception of it has to be
> measured as recorded history between two or more points separated in
> time.

Memory is fallible and records made at different points in time are less so. A
record in this case could be just a diary of major events.

The group as a system

When a group is labelled a 'system', what is actually meant? In order to answer
this we have to go back to the beginning. When a number of individuals gather
together, as individuals do in many aspects of our society, they have a perception about the nature of the company in which they find themselves. This perception varies from the purely coincidental fact of being close to one another in
physical space before separating a short time later with no sense of permanence
or even of value attaching to the meeting, to collections of individuals who

choose to stay together or who find themselves locked into a group by force of circumstances for long or short periods of time. These latter individuals possess some sense of belonging to a group, or of being contained in it, of being part of it and to some extent committed to it.

So our first definition of what a group system is is that it is composed of a number of individuals who spend significant amounts of time in each other's presence, have some sense of belonging and thus of being separate from others who are not members, and they may well have a common purpose(s) for being there. For comparative purposes, the *Collins Concise English Dictionary* (1988) defines 'system' as 'a group or combination of interrelated or interacting elements forming a collective entity; . . . any assembly of . . . components with interdependent functions, usually forming a self-contained unit'.

So a group of individuals may be considered to be a system when its elements (i.e. the individuals) are interrelated, interdependent or interactive with one another in such a way that they form a recognizable entity. As we are concerned here with the influences which operate within groups, we must realize that there is a difference between what our definition would call elements, discrete individuals and those individuals who are dependent upon each other, are interrelated or who interact with one another. The difference is usually a matter of opportunity, desire, need and time.

Thus we must look at two very different kinds of influence within groups: first, there are those influences which create a group system from a collection of discrete individuals; and, second, there are influences which operate within the group formed by the first influences to enable it to work or which, alternatively, break it down into its component parts (i.e. individuals).

In Chapter 2, we considered which factors or influences create groups, and so here we concentrate on those influences which operate within already formed groups, for if we can begin to see how these work we will have gone a long way towards understanding how groups work and how it becomes possible to influence what they can achieve. At the outset, we must try to simplify why people stay in groups having once joined or created them, or have found themselves in a group as part of a developing situation. So let us start with some very simple statements, which will need to be modified and fine-tuned later:

1. Being in any social situation creates costs and rewards for the individual.
2. In such situations, individuals will generally seek to maximize the rewards or diminish the costs or both.
3. To maximize rewards implies being able to gain from the social situation an acceptable degree of satisfaction.
4. To diminish costs may involve a withdrawal of effort or commitment or, alternatively, an increase to bring about a more satisfying situation.
5. The extreme method of diminishing costs in a social situation is created by leaving it altogether.

6. Freedom to leave may be either impossible or entail such cost that to remain is the only option – this may produce hostile or apathetic individuals.

Costs and rewards

If the above statements are related specifically to membership of a group, then all the effort, commitment, time and resources devoted to the group will be seen as costs, as will the alternative uses to which these efforts could have been directed and all the other situations which have been foregone. In some ways, the pleasure, satisfaction, gain, achievement, etc., which being a member of a particular group brings about, may be seen as rewards.

These costs and rewards are not only individually experienced, they are also linked to a number of other factors. If an individual is considering joining an existing group, then he or she can assess whether that group will meet his or her requirements – at least in so far as such an assessment of what may be a complex organization is possible. Thus individuals can choose both between various groups apparently offering similar rewards or whether to join at all.

On the other hand, where a group is just coming into existence, its potential members have no such access to information. However, what they may have is knowledge of other similar groups, or the idea that only a group specifically created to meet their requirements will serve their purpose. But consider their predicament – what they think they require is not available to them, and so they have to create such a group. Herein lies the possible application of one of the major skills of an effective groupworker, whose expertise is knowing how groups can be created from a collection of individuals and how the elements of group creation can be most effectively used to meet the specific needs of such individuals. Such a worker should also possess some knowledge about how long such an enterprise will take, and some skill in maintaining individuals' interest in the group until the rewards of the group become self-evident to its members.

The expectations of members

We are now in a position to look at those influences which create such groups and to modify our previous bald statements. Setting aside the basic need all human beings have for being in the presence of others, most groups are created to meet general and specific needs. Thus the first factor in the possible creation of a group is often the *expectation* that it might provide genuine help which is not apparently available from other sources or in other ways. However, in some created groups, this is not the first base. Many people have no thought that a group may help because either previous experience of group existence has not demonstrated such a possibility or, more likely, because a group has never been thought of as a possible answer to a problem for the simple reason that no knowledge of such a process exists.

What individuals who are joining a group usually require is information regarding how to gain access to resources, which will help them with whatever need or want they perceive themselves to have. This may be a simple need such as companionship, or a much more serious need. So the first major influence within the group stems from:

> The expectation of potential members that the group can provide some help at a cost the individual is prepared to pay.

Once the group begins to function, then each member will continue to assess its value in relation to the costs he or she has to bear. Of course, this is an over-simplification, because we cannot assess individual costs and rewards in the same way that we can assess them in relation to material goods. This is because there is no universally accepted exchange rate, a task performed by money in the field of economics. Also, during the process of maturation, individuals learn about 'deferred gratification', which in essence means that to postpone immediate rewards often produces more and better rewards some time in the future. This is a good thing for groupworkers, because they are able to use this knowledge as the basis for gaining time for the group to develop to the point where it can demonstrate a capacity to reward its members adequately and thus prevent their leaving for some alternative which appears to offer more for less.

When members can see that their expectations are being – or will be – met within a group, they will generally maintain their commitment to the group. Then, as the group becomes more of an entity, that commitment may well increase. What brings this about is the realization that the group has become a relatively 'safe' place and therefore that it is worth offering some energy, support and resources without undue risk of being hurt or rebuffed. How does this come about? It is usually generated by two other major influences: time and experience.

Time and experience

As a group continues to exist over a period of time, one thing that occurs automatically is that each individual member becomes increasingly aware of how the others in the group behave and how he or she responds to them. It becomes a matter of record how the group and the individuals within it handle the behaviour which occurs. Thus members quickly learn what kind of behaviour is generally acceptable, what is on the fringes of acceptability and what is definitely frowned upon. As we have noted elsewhere, these ratings of the group's standards of behaviour are individual, personal and derived from direct observation of, and participation in, the group as a system. They may have been outlined at some stage by a knowledgeable group leader, but such verbal information carries nothing like the same credibility which attaches to direct personal observation and assessment.

> Time spent within a group tends to generate a perception in each individual member of the standards of acceptable and unacceptable behaviour.

In essence, operating with a reasonable degree of satisfaction and safety within a group is dependent upon each member being able to predict with some accuracy the response patterns within that group.

Differences between members

Although a lot of groups are formed by people who believe that they have something in common – a common problem, interest or need – what tends to be the working material of a group usually turns out to be not so much the apparent similarity which brought them together in the first place, but how they differ one from another.

Because an individual with a problem related to loneliness joins a group of seven or eight others who also have found loneliness to be a problem, this does not mean that they are at all alike in many other aspects of their lives. Their loneliness will have arisen from a variety of causes, ranging from the self-inflicted to the unavoidable loss; their responses to it will be individual and different.

It is when these differences are able to emerge within the group, largely because its members feel that it is safe to talk about themselves, that the basic resources of the group also emerge. Not only does each member of such a group possess credibility in the eyes of the other members because of their experience, they also begin to realize that support and understanding is forthcoming, and above all a slot to fit into. There is also the fact that from difference can emerge new and different ideas about what one might be able to do, which had previously never even been dreamed of.

> Apparent similarity may be the foundation of many groups, but it is revealed difference which tends to create the most resources.

So our system contains elements which interact with each other and are interdependent, and which is definable both by its members and by external

Table 9 Influences at work in groups

Influence	Outcome
1. Cohesiveness	The influence a group exerts on its members to remain members
2. Attractiveness	The indicator of member satisfaction
3. Means control	The ability of the group to achieve ends which are important to members
4. Internal power	The ability of a group to induce changes
5. Activities	The group controls a wide range of activities
6. Credibility	The group engenders trust and provides expertise
7. Relevance	The group relates directly to the needs of members
8. Contagion	The way feelings spread among members
9. Frequency of contact	Generates intimacy and familiarity
10. Level of visibility	Shows members ways of doing things
11. Time	Allows development
12. Size	The effect of numbers to support and confirm
13. Roles	To offer practical resources
14. Closeness to real life	To offer a practice reality which is directly transferable to ordinary existence
15. Sub-groups	To be sources of innovation; to develop relationships and to contain differences
16. Norms and standards	To establish rules of behaviour and process
17. Conformity	To generate safety and containment
18. External factors	To develop responses to threat

observers as an entity in its own right – a group. Thus members have access to resources which they believe are necessary to meet their needs, even if this is just the presence of others who are deemed to be compatible, or others whose experience of some aspect of life offers the possibility of understanding based in that experience.

The list in Table 9 is a big one, but it is by no means exhaustive. However, as some of the influences listed were dealt with in Chapter 4 (e.g. cohesiveness, roles, conformity and interaction), and some are factors which occur constantly throughout this text, we will deal here with credibility, contagion, visibility, status, sub-groups, norms, time and external influences, and add some brief comments on conformity.

Credibility

An influence which has a very widespread effect is credibility. In a way, everyone knows exactly what 'credibility' means (i.e. that someone or something is believable), but it is also obvious that there are more powerful factors operating than are covered by this simple statement.

When individuals find themselves faced with uncertainty, when their own methods and ideas for coping with situations – both public and private – have demonstrably failed, there is a strong tendency to seek assistance. The essential qualities of that assistance which will make it acceptable are that it is available and that it appears to be valid. What is the essence of that validity?

In very simple terms, it resides in the perception that the potential helper actually understands the situation in which the distressed individual exists, and has some different ideas and methods to apply to the problem. Note that this does not imply that the helper actually has this understanding, merely that there is a belief that it exists. Indeed, the greater the desperation, the more likely that such a belief will occur where it is not warranted, if the need for help becomes desperate enough.

There are at least two kinds of understanding of particular human situations, one where a person has actually experienced a situation and survived. This is the basis of credibility of Alcoholics Anonymous and other self-help groups. The second kind of understanding is not dependent upon personal experience of a particular situation, but upon the accumulation and analysis of data about it. Credibility also rests upon a perception that individuals have developed methods of coping which have had demonstrable degrees of success in dealing with particular situations.

As an influence in a group, credibility tends to work in the area of generating trust – credible people know what they are doing and their actual presence, appearance and behaviour are acceptable evidence of this. They indicate that it is possible to overcome difficulties, to find methods of coping and to survive. The difficulty that experts (the second kind of 'credibles') often have is that their knowledge and experience appear less valid if they have not actually experienced the problem with which they are offering to deal. On the other hand, their knowledge is always wider and less personalized than would be arrived at by direct experience alone.

One of the problems a newcomer to a group always faces is the lack of evidence of credibility, unless it takes the form of 'reputation'; but for most people, credibility rests upon a belief fostered by observation and experience or upon dire need.

The effect of contagion

It may seem unusual to find a section in a book on groups entitled 'The effect of contagion'. But contagion is the best way to describe exactly what appears to happen. In the case of an infectious disease, for example, it is passed from one person to another by processes of contact in some form or other, and this is exactly what seems to happen in groups, though what is passed on is even less objectively tangible than disease entities.

We know that powerful emotions like fear and panic can spread like wildfire when masses of individuals, even though they are wholly unaware of the original cause of the fear or panic, are triggered into feeling those emotions by the reactions of those about them. The same process operates on a smaller scale with emotions and sensations which occur within a group. They operate at all levels, from very powerful feelings of anger, hatred, loathing and distrust all the way through to love, affection, security and warmth.

The main influence produced by contagion within a group is a form of conformity, which can often produce actions and participation in deeds which the individuals who comprise the group would never actually perform on their own. Sometimes these actions are regretted at a later date, but in many cases they serve to show individuals that being carried along by group feeling, being a part of the group, enables them to discover abilities and possibilities which they would not otherwise have dreamed were possible.

Example

When parents became part of the consultation process during the implementation of the All Wales Strategy for the Mentally Handicapped, a problem arose which related to the apparent inability of parents to make their points to groups containing specialist professionals. The professionals tended to consider the contributions made by the parents too individualistic and centred in their own limited personal experience and thus not directly applicable to the more global themes of the strategy.

This situation changed when parents' groups were given some help in preparing and presenting their material. With great trepidation, several parents from these groups faced groups of professionals and were eminently more successful than on previous occasions. The effect on the parents' groups was quite electric, as they were flushed with success and began to believe that they could now make their contributions and be accepted.

For a while this was true and contagion from success operated well, but then the scenario changed and the parents' groups once more experienced contagion, but this time it was negative and related to failure.

Visibility in groups

What becomes apparent to any group member who takes the time to stop and think about it, is that any individual in a small group is extremely visible to all the other members. In discussion of the effects of the different sizes of groups, one factor which emerges consistently is the fact that in small face-to-face groups there is nowhere that members can conceal themselves – there is no place to hide.

This is very frightening to some people, especially if the goodwill and acceptance of the group is important to them. The idea that their every move, their appearance, their utterances, gestures and body movements are all visible, can be threatening. Of course, there are individuals who relish being centre-stage with an audience watching them, but there are many others to whom it is an ordeal which can only be tolerated because they have a belief that it is either necessary or that some substantial reward will occur as a result of submitting oneself to such a process.

If visibility can be such an ordeal, wherein does its influence lie? Generally, its influence is two-fold. First, consciousness of exposure causes individuals to be mindful of the image they present and of the feedback that they receive in response to that presentation. As familiarity with the group and its processes develops, then that presentation can change, caution is relaxed and the fear of being exposed as the kind of person one would not like to be reduces. Thus the second influence lies in the fact that it does not take long for many members to realize that other group members are exposed to them. So over a period of time, it is possible for each member of a group to build up a picture of his or her colleagues. Hopefully, this image is not one which congeals at an early level of information and assessment, but one which is constantly adjusted in the light of new evidence personally observed.

It is only as part of this process that the resources represented by the members of the group become part of each member's understanding. And it is only through this process that a relevant level of trust of others can be developed, for it must be remembered that the evidence of one's own eyes and of one's own experience is considered to be a much more dependable source than any words can be. It must also be remembered in this context that any observed discrepancy between what is said and intended, and what actions actually follow, is a potent source of mistrust. In groupwork terms, this is 'dissonance', and what generates trust is 'consonance' between statement and behaviour – that is, agreement between words and action.

The status of members

The standing of an individual member in a group is based upon the group's assessment of his or her value, both as a person and as a group asset. Status can therefore change as perceptions change and is therefore different from authority, which may derive from a source outside the group or depend upon the possession of a particular role or rank. The legitimacy of a member's standing in the group is related to the way in which it was acquired – in effect, by the fact that it is acknowledged by the other members and its continuation is almost entirely dependent upon the behaviour of the high standing member from then on.

As an influence within a group, the following should be noted about high status:

1. It allows such members to influence others.
2. It permits them to behave in non-conforming ways to a greater extent than is allowed those of lesser standing, but only if such behaviour eventually either creates or is accompanied by some clearly observable benefit for the group as a whole.

3. It tends to put them in a position central to the communication system of the group and thus to decide the quality and quantity of information available to others.
4. It may provide for the exploitation of others and also for self-enhancement.
5. It may cause individuals to be the focus of the formation of sub-groups (see next section).
6. High status members tend to be more productive of new ideas and efforts for change than others.
7. It is usually associated with members who are perceived by others as being able to reward, support and reinforce them.
8. It tends to confer protection against challenge by other members as long as the high status member is seen as valuable.

Diagrammatically, high standing members can be represented as central to the group with clusters and sub-groups in close attendance; members of low status would then be shown at some distance from the centre with fewer connections to others, peripheral and in some cases isolated. It is not too strong a statement to say that high standing group members influence the way a group works, what it tries to do and in general they set the tone for all aspects of group behaviour. Conversely, members of low standing have much less effect upon a group, but are nevertheless the major operators of group policies and strategies initiated by members of high standing. An interesting form of low standing member, but who is extremely valuable to the group, is the 'scapegoat' (see Chapter 7).

Sub-groups – groups within groups

All systems are composed of separate elements operating in a pattern of relationships. A group is a system of individuals who operate in just such a relationship over a period of time. However, over a certain size and depending to a large extent on the purpose of the system, it is possible to discern within the larger system a series of smaller systems with some degree of autonomy of function.

Sub-groups are thus definable small systems within the larger group and they form for all manner of reasons (e.g. similarity of aims, personal liking, similar interests, etc.). They also vary between permanent alliances (e.g. a group of friends) and very transient ones set up in order to pursue certain aims within the group, which disintegrate as soon as the defined purpose is achieved or dropped.

Some sub-groups become very powerful by virtue of their ability to persuade others in the group to go along with their ideas. Indeed, any long-standing sub-group or combination of powerful members in a group can form a considerable power bloc which influences what the group does and how it does it. Thus a snag as far as new members in a group are concerned is that such powerful sub-groups do not necessarily advertise their presence and may well manipulate group decisions in ways which are not obvious until a new member has had time to observe the process for him or herself.

Table 10   The formation and influences of sub-groups

The main reasons for forming sub-groups are:
 1. Common interests, values and attitudes
 2. Physical proximity
 3. Perception of similar individual attributes (e.g. age, race, intelligence, culture, gender, ability, etc.)
 4. Collusion in order to meet similar needs
 5. Focal viewpoint which attracts satellites
 6. Security needs
 7. Pressure for minority representation
 8. During a process of gradual integration into a larger group
 9. Feelings of liking for individual members
10. Similarity of background and experience
11. Previous acquaintanceship or friendship

The main influences of sub-groups:
 1. Can enhance the total quality of the group
 2. May be the major focus of change in the group
 3. They can fragment the group effort through diffusing interest
 4. Can help establish the levels of standing within the group
 5. Can reduce the dependence of individuals on the group
 6. Can be a major source of new ideas

A method of checking what sub-groups exist is to be alert to the way members support one another in discussion. Note, for example, which group members offer ideas, suggestions and relevant information and which other members support them, and then check these factors against any decisions which may be reached. It is often the case that in some groups like committees, decisions are reached and agreed and quite a large number of the committee members may have no real idea how the decisions were arrived at. They simply did not see the sub-groups exercising their power.

Norms

Any collection of people working together for a period of time will appear to operate to a set of rules. Of course, if what they are doing is highly specialized in some way, then extra, new and different rules may eventually have to be formulated. Table 11 provides a brief summary of where rules of behaviour come from and the effects they can have on the groups's performance.

The term 'norm' is used in groupwork to indicate 'rules' which are established on the basis that they describe generally accepted forms of behaviour, whereas the term 'rule' itself tends to be used when acceptable behaviour patterns have been made explicit and formalized, either in verbal or written form.

Table 11   Sources and effects of rules

The sources of the rules system within a group:
1. The general rules of behaviour of the society and community in which the group exists
2. Learning derived from experience within the group
3. Any stated rules which the group may have produced (e.g. ground rules)
4. The expectations of members
5. Conformity pressures
6. The fundamental assumptions and beliefs of members
7. The influence of leaders, dominant members and any organization of which the group may be a part

The effects of this system of rules:
1. It tends to create a frame of reference, against which members know where they stand
2. It tends to reduce risks by increasing regularities, predictability and stability
3. It helps to determine major aspects of the group's function
4. It creates boundaries within which special abilities and efforts at change can start from a secure base
5. It creates a framework with which new members can come to terms
6. It reduces possible requirements for external control
7. It can also increase resistance to change by operating as an inflexible tradition
8. It creates a standard against which deviance can be measured
9. It creates a control of behaviour factor
10. It increases the possibility of conforming behaviour

The influence of norms is immense, because they express the consensus of group members, control behaviour and are frequently enforced by forms of punishment for transgression, which can range from exclusion and ignoring through reprimand to eviction. Some groups punish defaulters by physical means, mutilation and death (e.g. the para-military groups of Northern Ireland), whereas others maintain their form of discipline through fear.

Conformity

Some discussion has already taken place with regard to this particular influence (see Chapter 2), but there are still some important aspects yet to be presented. As we noted earlier in this chapter, deviation from the generally accepted patterns of behaviour, except for members of high standing, tends to result in some form of punishment. The power of conformity to influence group outcomes depends on it being able to introduce order into group behaviour and thus to ensure that the behaviour of individual members is coordinated to achieve maximum success in the group endeavour. It also tends to reduce friction, because individual members are no longer singled out and pressurized to conform.

But there are still certain problems to consider. Conformity may be more apparent than real, in which case it is often referred to as 'public' conformity. It is nevertheless still a powerful influence on group behaviour, despite the fact that as the term suggests it is a process which an individual sets in motion purely to reduce the pressure on him or her to comply with group norms. It is a security measure, but although the individual who cooperates publicly may not agree in private with what is going on, for the purposes of the group it is given whole-hearted support. A problem arises when the task of the group is to effect lasting change in individual members, for unless full private acceptance is involved, little actual change will occur that outlasts the life of the group or an individual's membership of it.

There are several factors which are known to affect the level of conformity in a group (see Table 12). However, it must be remembered that the summaries of complex behaviour shown in Table 12 are but rough guides to probable outcomes. Differences of group structure and of the abilities and experience of members can ensure significant differences to the general conclusions given here.

Time

It cannot have escaped the reader's notice that throughout this book there are constant references to time and to processes which take time to manifest themselves. So one of the major influences in a group is the passage of time, or the limits to time in which things must be done.

If group processes can be described as patterns or repetitive behaviours, then they can only be truly seen as such over a period of time. For instance, it is neither logical nor efficient to make assessments of the resources which a group of individuals might possess until there is some basic demonstration by those individuals of what might be available. Because such demonstrations occur in ordinary everyday life, most of us have some knowledge of what resources we have access to. But in each new group, that starting of knowledge has to be expanded in two ways. First, in selecting from our own resources and then in exploring the potential which might develop from them and second from an appraisal of the resources available or potentially available from our fellow group members. Such an appraisal can only take place over time, for our initial assumptions need to be modified in the light of experience and the changes which such appraisals bring about.

Where time is in short supply, then it must be realized that this imposes strict limits upon what can be achieved. It also imposes the necessity of using group methods which are best suited to limited time-spans. Thus it is wholly inappropriate for a group facing a short life-span to use techniques which lack structure and discipline and depend to a large extent upon the development of firm trusting relationships. Much more appropriate would be a clear definition of ends, the allocation of various tasks to named individuals, a time schedule which

Table 12 Factors which influence the level of conformity

Factor	Outcome
Public/private acceptance	The degree to which members operate to achieve an individual level of safety, or the level at which they accept the need for and possibility of change
Commitment	The amount of energy and effort which members are prepared to put into achieving group aims; usually, the greater the belief in the group, the greater the level of conformity
Attractiveness of group	Usually, the more attractive a group is to its members, the greater the level of conformity
Status	High status allows members to behave in deviant ways, providing it benefits the group; thus it is usually middle status members whose conformity levels are the highest
Interdependence	Where members are greatly dependent upon each other for support and resources, then conformity is usually high
Group composition	Too many obvious dissimilarities in the membership of a group tends to reduce conformity; equally, consistent and all-pervading similarity produces conformity to a level of stagnation
Size	Small groups, allowing for other factors, have a higher record of achieving conformity than larger ones
Norms	Where the normally acceptable behaviour of a group is close to what most of its members would expect, conformity is relatively high; however, where the norm is extreme, then conformity may be difficult to achieve
Group competence	Where a group demonstrates an ability to cope with the task for which it was established, then conformity is usually at a high level
Confidence	The level of confidence of members of a group usually equates with the level of conformity
Difficulty of the group task	If a group's task is perceived by its members as extremely difficult and there is little evidence of successful coping, then conformity levels will tend to drop; if, however, the need to accomplish the task is of great importance to all members, then this may be sufficient to ensure a high level of public conformity

indicated when results were required and a fallback plan should circumstances prevent the original schedule being achieved, and most certainly a clear directive leadership which served to eliminate from the proceedings all side issues and apparent irrelevancies, however tempting.

Conversely, where time is not a factor, then goals which are concerned with a steady growth of personal awareness and the development of interdependence can be considered. Such is the power of time, that if it is not considered when working in groups, it will force certain issues on to the agenda whether they are what the group wants or not.

External influences

If we regard a group as a system, then it also has to be remembered that as sub-groups are small systems within groups, groups themselves are sub-systems within larger groups or organizations. No matter how loose this embedding may be, the influence of the world outside filters through the group boundaries and the group's influence filters outwards. Indeed, as we have seen, most members of specific groups only enter the group situation for very limited periods of time, and bring with them the concerns and experiences in which they are currently involved.

Small groups which are a part of a larger organization are influenced by the ideals, purposes, policies, etc., of the larger organization, especially if they were created to deal specifically with some selected aspect of that larger organization's work. Thus terms of reference may have been established, and deliberate goals and personnel chosen. This direct form of external influence is easy to comprehend, because it is built into the group as it is created. But it must also be remembered that groups feed influence outwards into the larger organization and are sometimes instrumental in bringing about considerable change. Some small groups established within large organizations are given the brief to define areas of change and also to devise means of achieving it.

But some external influences are neither so obvious nor so direct. The actual environment, the surroundings in which a group exists, can exert significant influence on its performance levels, and yet that influence may never be wholly recognized for what it is. For instance, a group may work in physical surroundings which are depressing, frustrating and so productive of problems that the group has little time to devote to its real task for coping with them. Buildings may remind group members of previous work environments – good or bad – which may promote attitudes to their current group's work which may not be wholly appropriate.

The simple rule to remember is that however powerful or absorbing a group experience may be, the environment in which it exists and from which its members come will have some effect upon the group's performance.

No group exists in a vacuum, nor are its members able to free themselves of the act of importing and exporting influences across group boundaries.

Summary of main points

1. The influence a group can exert is directly related to the members' need for the group.
2. A group is a system of actual and potential human resources.
3. Time is an essential element in the development of a group.
4. The relative standing of group members affects the degree of influence they can exert.
5. All groups contain sub-groups and most groups are themselves sub-groups embedded in larger groups or organizational systems.
6. Norms are the standards both explicit and hidden by which the group operates.
7. Conformity when brought about by group influence may be either public, which is usually a personal security measure, or private, which implies wholehearted agreement, even when no influence is exerted.

List of basic concepts and terms

Influence: pressure which can affect members' behaviour.
Group members' behaviour: tends to be governed by individual perception of cost and reward.
Expectations: individuals become members of groups with their own ideas about what will happen and what they would like to happen.
Experience: members bring their experience of other group situations and use this as a standard of assessment.
Time: essential for the group to 'form'.
Member differences: the basic potential group resource.
Credibility: the basis of group trust.
Contagion: emotions, ideas and feelings spread quickly in a group because of the physical closeness of members and also because of pressures to conform.
Visibility: small groups in particular, but most groups in practice, create a situation in which members are clearly exposed to one another.
High status: in a group this is usually related to members' perception that an individual is of great value to the group.
Embedding: all groups contain smaller groupings and are themselves usually embedded in larger groups.

Topics for discussion

1. Take any group of which you are member and draw up a list of the sub-groups it contains. Check carefully to note those members who are in several different sub-groups and those who appear to be in only one, or even none at all.
2. What are the observable effects of (a) multiple sub-group membership and (b) virtual isolation?
3. In a group you know well, try to define clearly the rules by which it operates. Can you spell out the differences between the formal explicit rules of the group and the informal implicit rules.
4. How do members discover what the informal implicit rules are?
5. How long does it take?
6. Trust is often quoted as a very necessary element in a functioning group. How would you define it?
7. What kind of trust do you think is necessary for a new group in which its members are strangers and independent professionals.

Reading list

The influences operating within a group have been defined by writers of many different persuasions in social psychology; thus some reference to some factors will be found in any general text. Most of the ideas mentioned here will be found in the following:

Raven, B.H. and Rubin, J.Z. (1976). *Social Psychology: People in Groups*. John Wiley: New York.

Collins, B.E. and Guetzkow, J.Z. (1964). *A Social Psychology of Group Processes for Decision-making*. John Wiley: New York. This text, while primarily concerned with the way decisions are made in groups, also covers matters like interpersonal relations, sources of power and influence, communication in interaction, satisfaction and leadership.

Baron, R.S., Kerr, N. and Miller, N. (1992). *Group Process, Group Decision, Group Action*. Open University Press: Buckingham. This text includes chapters on individual/group performance, which cover resources, social influence and conformity, decision-making, cooperation, and conflict and aggression.

6 Presentation, perception, communication, difference and resources

Introduction: why it is necessary for group members to have some
understanding of the topics of this chapter
Observation: Looking and seeing and the problem of interpretation
Self-presentation: How we think of ourselves and how we appear to others
Perception of others: how others appear to us
The perception of difference
Differences:
• Background
• Culture
• Race
• Beliefs
• Power
• Gender
• Expectation
• Ageism
Discrimination and oppression
Differences as resources
Causes of failure to communicate

Introduction

In Chapter 7, we will look at the processes of entering a group, remaining a member and getting out. In preparation for these exercises, this chapter discusses some of the major social issues which affect the ways individuals see, accept or reject one another and which therefore affect not just how comfortable a member and a group are with each other, but also how in the long term the members affect the functioning of the group.

In the past, much has been made about the process of joining an established group (see the references to newcomers later) and the problems of integration. But almost without exception they were based upon the assumption that both the newcomer and the group shared a common background. Since then, there has been a growing recognition that such similarity and homogeneity may have been a myth even then and that it certainly is so now. So added to the universal problems of entry into a group, it is now necessary to consider other issues of difference.

Some of the most important factors involved are perceptions of worth, the perception of the possession of power and its use, and the effects of powerlessness. Into this must come some understanding of the difference between self-rating and other-rating, of expectations and stereotyping processes, the perceptions relating to gender and what constitutes prejudice. Many other expectations are also involved, including those which relate to culture, background and experience. In a multiracial society, they all have to be reckoned with. Discrimination is nothing new in our society, but it has many more targets currently and a great deal of hostility appears to be involved.

Because we are considering the effects of differences, it is essential that the immense resources which can lie in differences should be scrutinized as should some of the problems of communication. The latter is important, because we tend to take for granted the fact that we *can* communicate effectively, which tends to blind us to the deficiencies inherent in our verbal communication system, especially in areas related to feelings.

Finally, there are those factors which relate to oppressive and suffocating behaviour.

Observation: looking and seeing and the problem of interpretation

As with communication, which we will deal with later in this chapter, we have a strong tendency to believe that seeing is something which we do naturally and involves no skill whatsoever. However, no-one asks another to match colours by recalling mentally what they were. We know that individual perceptions of colour are significantly different, and that this is even more true when what we are observing is not a simple fact like colour but complex human behaviour. So what are the problems of observation?

The first problem relates to who is doing the observing. For instance, if you are involved in an action as the actor, then your recall of what you saw will tend to be dictated by the fact that you believe that what you did was a response to the situation as you found it. If you are a bystander who is not involved in the action, you will tend to think that what the actor did was dictated by the kind of person he or she was. This can produce very different accounts of the same piece of action.

> Observing is not a mere mechanical activity. It always involves selection and interpretation.

The main drive in selection may well be interest. For instance, when people are asked to recall what they remember of a situation, a large part of the reported differences relate to which aspects of the situation held their attention and interest. Another factor which tends to promote attention is perception of threat or the bizarre and unusual. It is quite usual for individuals not to recognize people they know very well if they are met in unusual and unexpected circumstances.

Interpretation crucially depends upon the way we have learned to construe the world and thus also to experience it. Most of what we accept as 'natural' about our environment and the behaviour of ourselves and others (which becomes part of our system of making sense of our world) we have actually *learned*. Thus for a group member to become an effective observer of what is going on in the group, there is a need to:

1. Be prepared and to pay conscious attention to the process of 'seeing' (i.e. treat it as a skill to be acquired).
2. Be aware to some extent of the interpretative system which is being used. In effect, this means being aware of the 'constructs' we use to make sense of our world, which put another way would mean being aware of our biases.
3. Know what aspects of behaviour are likely to attract considerable attention and thus detract from attention paid to less likely attractors.

Decisions to act or not to act, about how to respond to others, are based upon our interpretation of what we see occurring before us, and as we have just noted those interpretations are in themselves formed from idiosyncratic past experience and highly personal constructs. If a group member is aiming for some realistic understanding of what goes on in his or her group, then some upgrading of observational skills is imperative.

Differences of interpretation are crucial differences. They are the basis for expanding the possible approaches to problems and aims, but they are also the basis of much misunderstanding, especially when the differences remain undisclosed. When this happens, the different behaviour – seen from the point of view of the observer – tends to be attributed to the personality of the actor and criticism of it is often framed in this way, much to the annoyance of the actor.

> What a group member does not see cannot be taken into that member's understanding of the group's process. But without doubt those unseen and unaccounted-for factors will still influence the group's outcomes.

Self-presentation: how we think of ourselves and how we appear to others

Interaction between group members (i.e. the way they react to each other) is based upon two major perpetual factors. The first revolves around the way we think of ourselves, plus how we believe others see us, and the second is concerned with the ways in which we see others.

Our ideas about ourselves tend to be built up over time into a relatively stable image that usually only changes when we are confronted with an inescapable awareness that this image is no longer even reasonably true. The major sources of information which we use to construct this self-image and sustain it reside in noting the way others, especially important others, react to us. This is essentially a form of categorization which others apply to us, in the same way that we tend to categorize them. The reactions of others is then based upon this categorization and in time we come to anticipate that this is how we are seen and to accept ourselves in these terms.

One's self-image is also formed when we compare ourselves to others. We constantly receive information from competing with others, from feedback about our performance and behaviour, and the effects we have on them. This is particularly true about those with whom we are in long-term contact, for instance family members. The roles we play also tend to shape self-image. For instance, many people, when asked to define themselves, do so in terms of the job they do and in terms of their expectation of how such a role should be performed.

Another source of image-forming material comes from the way we sometimes strive to be like someone else, usually a person we admire. In adolescence, there is often a strong urge and need to find an identity, to discover a consistent personality and many decisions about self-image are made. The inadequate formation of a self-image tends to result in confusion about self and in low self-esteem, which in turn generates problems in the area of achievement.

The way we think about ourselves tends to condition how we behave in the presence of others, because we have expectations of how we will be received and are able to anticipate how a given situation will unfold even before we get into it. When these expectations are largely realized, this then confirms our self-image. When they are not realized, a degree of confusion may arise, because, by implication, either others are wrong in their perception of and response to us or we are wrong in some major aspect of our self-image. This is one of the reasons why we try to ignore those people we believe will not actually confirm our view of ourselves.

There is yet another complicating factor, which is that as well as the self-image built upon stored feedback from others and the other sources we have just discussed, there is also an ideal image which is essentially based upon what we would like to be like. This is a personal construct and may well be in contradiction to both our ordinary self-image and the responses made to us by others.

The experience of some individuals has meant they consider themselves to be of very little worth due to a process of consistent denigrating and derogatory feedback. Indeed, society frequently and deliberately creates social roles for some groups by a process of consistently diminishing their self-esteem, a process which also generates prejudice against them in other areas of the society not directly affected.

Perception of others: how others appear to us

Given that each person's perception of the other members of his or her group is individual to a large extent and therefore idiosyncratic, and having discussed briefly how this comes about, it is now essential for us look at the general process of person assessment, for without doubt all our actions in respect of others will have some basis in those perceptions.

Most information about others comes from what we see and what we hear. The sense of touch may also be involved peripherally. But whatever the distribution between sensory inputs may be, we interpret them and make inferences from them. This process of assessment and storage of information tends to be composed of material relating to the perceived personality, the expression of emotions and the attitudes on display.

A process of categorization takes place as we see and hear the aspects of an individual's personality being expressed. Usually, such categorization takes time, because material needs to accumulate before making an impact. Thus categorization tends to depend upon features of personality which are constant as, for instance, when we note that one individual remains cheerful under a variety of different situations. We note behaviour, we see physical clues and we hear comments from which we produce a 'personality' of inferred traits.

That this process takes place can be demonstrated when an individual who knows another very well notices that changes have taken place or that some particular action is 'out of character'. Change can only be detected by a comparison of the changed state with a previous stable pattern. Hence a perception of change implies the existence of a previous pattern.

Assessments can be affected by relational states. For instance, if one person has a strong dislike or a strong liking for another person, then the assessments such an individual will make are inevitably biased by that fact.

The cues which an individual tends to use are those which are presented early in the contact process, commonly referred to as 'first impressions'; those which strike the individual as the most vivid and those which occur with greater frequency.

The assessment of emotional evidence is a much more difficult process for the simple reason that individuals display considerable variation in the manner in which they express similar emotions. For instance, there are differences of expression of the same emotion by the same person at different times and in different circumstances; there are also differences of expression between individuals, classes and cultures, and other background circumstances also influence the ways in which similar emotions are expressed. There are also differences in the degree of awareness individuals have of the ways in which they express or control their emotions. The assessment process may also be constrained by the nature of the interaction in which the emotional expression occurs. For instance, the interaction may be one-way in nature, as in the giving of an order; it may be one in which both parties are involved, but one party is more dominant than the other; or it may be an interaction in which there is equality of participation. All these factors may affect the perceptions of one person by another.

Individuals handle incoming information about others in idiosyncratic ways because their personal constructs, the individual template against which information is compared and matched, have vastly different degrees of complexity and indeed different priorities. Other factors which influence information processing include superiority, dependence, age differentials, attitudes (e.g. friendly or aggressive), moods and previous information.

One thing which stands out here is that the way we interpret our perceptions of others is part of a very complex process. Such interpretation is often based upon an overall lack of adequate information on which to make an assessment. This is one good reason why the passage of time allows more information to be accumulated and first impressions to be modified.

The perception of difference

The discussion of difference presented here intends to demonstrate that what is regarded as strange is also seen as threatening and tends to elicit some form of protective and defensive behaviour. A common factor of many forms of social interaction is that the quality and quantity of information that individuals have about each other is neither good nor adequate. As we have seen in discussing self-presentation and the perception of others, we make assumptions, based on inadequate data, because most social situations require this kind of response.

We work, play and live with people in groups whom we may know very well in those situations because of long-term contact; however, we may know nothing about the much larger, more important parts of their lives conducted outside of the contact group. We also have a whole series of constructs and stereotypes which may also have been originally based on inadequate or defective material, but which are used as instruments to allow us to cope with meeting differences. However handy such constructs may be, they tend to have one thing in common: they seldom fit the people we apply them to, and in so doing generate a denial of their individuality.

There is a distinction to be made between becoming aware that an individual is different by reason of race or culture, for example, and categorizing that individual with the stereotypical picture commonly applied to the whole of that race or culture. The first is a recognition that a unique individual has been involved in a process of acculturation. Therefore, we note that the individual's behaviour, responses, value system, attitudes and opinions will be those appropriate to that process and of course different to our own. The second arises because the unique individual is ignored and he or she is credited with a set of general characteristics which, rightly or wrongly, are deemed to be common to all individuals who belong to that race or culture.

It is important to recognize that this process has been applied to people who are different, even if their point of origin is no more than a mile or so away from where everybody else in the group comes from. Where a lack of understanding exists about the reasons for the particular behaviour of an individual, then that gap in understanding will tend to be filled by assumptions. Almost inevitably those assumptions will relate much more accurately and strongly to the experience of the person making them, than to the individual about whom they are made. Because of this, they are usually wrong in some major aspect.

So there are two common approaches to the matter of difference. One relates to the individual, requiring that we respond to a distinct individual from a different background with understanding and acceptance, a process not dissimilar to the integration process of different individuals from the same background. The second stems from the realization that ethnic differences are not just the differences we see in one individual, but a much wider issue involving ideas of equal validity of people, and a host of attitudes and problems. It is also important to consider carefully any interpretations of behaviour which we make, especially because of the tendency we have to seek explanations in terms of personality characteristics and to attach labels.

Differences

Background

'Background' is a non-specific term which is used to cover all aspects of the milieu in which a person has grown and in which he or she still exists. It covers family, upbringing, education, experience and the environment in which an individual lives or has lived, all of which will have been instrumental in shaping behaviour patterns, beliefs, attitudes, opinions and expectations. Of course, some people move away from their original background, and they may even manage to eradicate some of the effects of it by a conscious effort of will, but the fact that they had to struggle against that background will mean that it was once a potent influence in at least a part of their lives, and may even continue to be.

Let us look briefly at two aspects of 'background' in an attempt to show us how people are literally programmed by it and how knowledge of 'background' generates expectations of a particular kind in others who become aware of it.

Educational attainment has consistently been used as a method of ensuring that an individual is able to obtain satisfactory employment and hence a reasonable standard of life. But not all people can achieve high standards of education, usually because they are unable to gain access to educational institutions or they are regarded as being incapable of taking advantage of what is on offer. The educational system is, by its very design, not suited to everyone, because some individuals learn in different ways.

Nevertheless, the expectation of what an individual can achieve is different if that individual is known to have had a 'good' education. There is an expectation that such a person will be intelligent and have learned how to think, will be able to express themselves clearly and to have a wider vision and understanding. This expectation may not be consonant with the known facts about some people who have had a 'good' education, but nevertheless it is still there in some form or other.

Experience is another aspect of 'background'. This can range from the experience of growing up in a particular area with a distinct set of beliefs and attitudes to society, to the experience of work in a particular job. Experience tends to be admired and accepted because it is something which is tangible and practical.

Differences usually present as pertaining to the individual, and herein lies a problem. There is no doubt that a response to perceived differences must initially be along individual lines, but it must also be borne in mind that many of the differences presented by an individual are not so much manifestations of personal idiosyncrasies as outcomes due to social forces which are political, economic or racial in nature.

If, for instance, an individual has grown up experiencing discrimination and poverty, to describe his or her more deviant attitudes and behaviours to society and its institutions as personal is to miss the point altogether. The form of expression such attitudes take can with some justice be described as personal or individual, but the attitudes themselves are created by the social processes to which the individual has been subjected. They are therefore environmental in nature.

Recognition of this simple fact may lead to an understanding of difference which can be used as the basis of resources (e.g. the use of experience; sharing; the common experience) and as the basis of the development of processes which have the potential of changing, if not the social factors involved as a whole, at least some part of those immediate pressures which arise from them and thus indirectly change the personal quality of life of those involved.

Culture

More specific than the general idea of background is the concept of 'culture', which generates some of the largest differences between human beings. A culture may be defined by the possession by its members of a shared language; a shared way of perceiving and thinking about the world in which they live (e.g. the perception of time varies between cultural traditions); agreed forms of non-verbal communication and of social interaction designed to make cooperation within the culture possible; rules and conventions about acceptable ways of behaving in a wide variety of situations; agreed standards and values, morals and usually a system of religious beliefs; a range of material skills and particular forms of technology.

Language is often the major difference between cultures, as it forms the basis of categorization, the kind of order that individuals impose upon the world in order to understand and cope with it. Some people are bilingual because they find themselves living in a country in which the language is not their mother tongue. However, one's most essential ideas and deepest feelings can usually still only find satisfactory expression in one's mother tongue, and thus they are extremely difficult to communicate to others not of the same culture.

Other cultural differences encompass varying levels of acceptance of aggression and achievement, and differences in social organization. When these differences are exported to another culture, the individuals who are steeped in them may recognize for the first time that they are different. But adaptation is a slow process for both sides, and the perception of the need for adaptation has to come from within the group itself rather than from any external pressure to change by the adoption of external values and patterns of behaviour.

Race

Differences in race are often obvious, which is itself a problem, in that by accepting obvious differences not so obvious differences can be ignored. For instance, ethnic groups have learned to be cautious about their reception in foreign countries because experience has taught them that racial prejudice, often containing strong elements of hostility, is usually present in some form or other, even though not immediately discernible. That caution can be interpreted by others at best as reluctance to join in organizations which are not specific to a particular ethnic group, and at worst as a culturally and racially defined hostility to mixed-race organizations.

Non-acceptance of the cultural rules of ethnic minorities is a conscious behaviour and deplorable, but ignorance of the fact that different cultural rules exist and mean as much to the individuals who abide by them as our rules do to us is an entirely different matter, however regrettable, and can only be resolved by a persistent and widespread programme of information.

Beliefs

In the UK, the influence of religion on behaviour, while still manifest in a large number of response patterns and thought processes, no longer forms an essential basis of the lifestyle of the majority of the population. But there are members of the indigenous population and incomers who have a much stronger compulsion to live by the dictates of their faith, not just regarding religious matters but everyday affairs as well. It is not an adequate response to suggest that such people, because they are resident in a society which does not consider such obedience to religious rules and rites important, that those who do should relinquish them and conform to the majority pattern.

Most incomers accept that the civil laws of the host country are to be obeyed, unless they are in direct conflict with some of the most important of their religious rites. But they claim, rightly, that their religious observances, when not in conflict with the civil law, are an essential part of their cultural identity and should be respected. Such matters as the role of women and children, matters of dress and patterns of social behaviour may all be dictated by religious law, and while they may seem not just different but archaic and oppressive to others, they are essentially cultural and group identity factors which are fundamental to being a member of that particular racial group.

Power

One of the most important differences that can be found in our society is that which exists between those who possess power and the ways in which they use it and those who are powerless. Power is not an easy concept to define, and in many cases its use as a term is not clearly visible. The individual exercise of power is one thing, but the power which sets agendas, defines serious social problems in particular ways, excludes and includes, is entirely different. Such a use of power is, if noticed at all, regarded as normal and traditional, and unless it comes to a head in the form of an individual personal negative experience, seldom challenged.

Until fairly recently, power has received very one-sided attention. Indeed, such attention has in general been concerned with defining power, which is a notoriously difficult thing to do. Some attention has been given to the ways in which people who have power tend to use it and to the actual origins of power. The other side of the coin, which is of much greater concern to a large number of people, is not concerned with the possession of power but with various degrees of the lack of it. This imbalance is in the process of being rectified. Both sides will be considered here for the simple reason that all human interaction has some element of influence involved in it and all group members should have some inkling of how power gambits are employed, both to enhance and develop personal resources and equally how they can be used to curtail or abort them or to inhibit development.

Powerlessness is a term which is used to define the state of individuals who have little or no control of large and important areas of their lives. Decisions about such areas are made without consultation or notice or, if notice is given, any response is usually ignored and those affected tend not to know of, or have access to, the systems which control them. A great deal of this applies to most people within a society for the simple reason that societies operate by offering certain areas of protection in return for the submission of individuals and groups to a set of laws and rules of behaviour. But within this general system, some people are much less able to take advantage of the security of society than others, and infinitely less able to compel it to conform even to its own rules than others. Such people, by virtue of their position within society, become objects rather than subjects and as a result develop negative self-evaluations which spill over into the general population, who regard them as stigmatized. Thus whatever skills and resources they possess are seldom either well used or even recognized to exist and the information they need to remedy this situation is not forthcoming.

Most of the major formulations of what power is tend to stem from the obvious, which is that power is usually seen as the ability of one person or a group of people to influence the behaviour of others both to the extent and in the direction they choose. The difficulty arises when an attempt is made to discover how such people and groups actually come to have that ability. Most theoreticians agree that in many cases power is actually given by some members of society to others, usually on the basis that those selected are able to operate for the benefit of all. Any society, however small or large, tends to legitimize power for some of its members in order that the group shall have some order and direction. If such giving of power does take place, then theoretically there is no reason why it should not be taken away in the same manner. But the strong hand of tradition and established practice lies heavily on such matters. Of course, those who attain positions of power come to realize that it has several advantages and are thus relatively reluctant to relinquish it.

Power is inevitably linked with the ability to induce change, so those with power can:

1. Initiate behaviour, thus bringing about change at the time and in the direction desired by the initiator.
2. Have greater freedom of action.
3. Use it to ensure the conformity of others with their views and values.
4. Gain more personal satisfaction from interaction with others.

The very structure of organizations creates power for some. Indeed, the function of organizations depends for its efficacy on this fact. If those without power in an organization see the possibility of rising to a position of power, then the value of that reward is such that unless obstacles are placed in their way, they will maintain the system's power structure because they hope to become part of it. In contrast to this kind of maintenance of power by virtue of hoping to become part of it, there is also the perception that a power system can punish. Power also adheres to those who are seen as possessing assets which the group or the community cannot do without, and power is handed to those we like.

What is so frustrating about these concepts of power is that if they are so easily given, why are they so difficult to rescind? Inertia may be an answer, but much more likely is the fact that even the process of giving power is little understood; it is not the will to rescind which is missing, but the practicality of how it can be done. Groups often provide the very first inkling for many people of the process of power development and decline.

Gender

Another obvious difference is that between the sexes. Group members are often aware that considerable change has taken place in the traditional roles of men and women in our society, and a degree of unease exists about what is acceptable behaviour and what is not. Indeed, for many people, the changes have the force of an idea which they know is current but which has not yet informed their behaviour; in other words, they are not convinced that it is wholly acceptable. This tends to engender some hostility, particularly among men, who see their traditional roles – strongly directed towards achievement, competition, performance and sexual competence, and not showing their feelings – being challenged. Their expectations, which as we will see later are a very potent component of action, are merged in perplexity and some curiosity about the changing nature of social relationships. This in turn has brought about a new expectation, that of a near-role reversal situation accompanied by some negative attitudes towards women and a degree of caution.

As is to be expected in an era when traditional roles are being examined and changed, this throws up other differences in the way in which individuals choose to deal with those changes. Most of what has been said here about self-perception and the perception of others applies with great force in this particular area of human relationships.

Expectation

As I have just noted, expectation, which may be defined as the perceptions we have of a situation before we enter into it, is another area of notable differences. We all make assumptions, often based on very deeply hidden constructs, about such essential things as 'normal' behaviour; about what is 'adequate' and what is 'acceptable'. If a society existed in which all of its members held the same assumptions, then there would be no problems. But no such society does or can exist. In any society, there are differences which have always warranted different kinds of treatment by the society as a whole. All societies have old people and young people, women and men, poor and rich; people of different ethnic background, people of different status, standing and power; people with different beliefs, both spiritual and political; people who are regarded as deserving and those who are not; the law-abiding and the law-breaking. All these groups and others are valued differently by the society in which they exist, some groups being over-valued and others hardly even tolerated.

The point of this argument is that when attitudes in a society change from an acceptance of the existing method of treating such groups to an attitude which begins to recognize that traditionally accepted views may be unjust, discriminatory, divisive, oppressive, cruel and demeaning, and in any case have not been seriously examined for far too long, changes begin to be made and tend to threaten long-standing behaviours. There is always a time-lag in the modification of a society's behaviour, and this is accompanied by a strong residual belief that the old ways may have had quite a lot to recommend them and indeed that the 'new' ways are just a fad that will soon pass.

In this way, during the period of transition from old to new, a significant number of the old views will still be felt to be 'natural' and will continue to form the basis of behaviour, although the ideas themselves are quite well hidden. Intellectually, people will grasp the value of 'new' ideas, but those which were current in their early years are likely to continue to have a very strong emotional input. How else can we explain racism and sexism and other forms of discriminatory behaviour so long after they were found to be unacceptable and after they have been legislated against?

Most of the factors we have considered as differences here are part of this process of changing attitudes in society. But it must be remembered that those who are regarded as 'different' by others have expectations themselves. They have learnt that despite so-called changes in social attitudes, they can still expect the residual factor to produce discrimination and hostility.

Another aspect of this matter of expectations concerns those assumptions that one group in a society have about another group which have not been made public, nor against which arguments of their inequality have been directed. The effect of these expectations is thus much more subtle by virtue of their hidden nature. The interaction processes of those who hold such assumptions are more difficult to condemn, because the sources are unknown to the holders, have never been questioned and are thus held to be 'natural'. The best we can expect is that when these assumptions which govern their behaviour stand revealed, they will change their public behaviour accordingly. Thus while black people may well have an expectation that they will be discriminated against in some way, many of those they will see as being discriminatory will be almost wholly unaware that what they are doing can be so regarded, because they will not have considered or reviewed their behaviour in the light of different social conditions from those which obtained when it was first developed.

Another factor which is involved in expectations is 'fear'. Like change, difference – especially extremely visible difference – can generate fear. The basis of such a response may well be that difference poses a challenge, a threat to the established and binding effects of traditional and accepted behaviour. After all, one of the most cohesive factors in any group is that large area of commonly held norms. Fear generated by difference can thus harden attitudes of solidarity for the traditional group and can generate attitudes of hostility and rejection, often with violent expression, towards those who are perceived as different. The expectation in these cases is that difference is not just 'different' but also wrong and unacceptable.

Ageism

In a society in which change occurs with increasing rapidity, the differences between age groups becomes much more marked. While adaptability to change, new ideas, new behaviours, values, inventions, etc., can serve to reduce the gap, the appetite for constant adaptation tends to diminish with increasing age. This may be due not so much to a lack of will, but to the reduced amount of energy older people have; what is there is essentially spent on the known and tested, rather than the new and different. For instance, most young people are computer-literate; most older people are not. This produces a whole area of difference in the perception of the way in which information is transmitted and indeed in what kind of information is actually of value.

Where change is not so rapid, the wisdom of age has always been regarded as relevant to the matters of current society. But in industrial and post-industrial societies, the knowledge accumulated with age and experience tends to be regarded as related to matters no longer of essential interest. It is to be expected that there may be clashes between individuals who come from societies in which the elderly are respected and those who live in societies which regard the elderly as a problem. All differences generate the likelihood of being regarded by others as 'irrelevant', particularly in those societies in which the 'current' – the 'here and now' – is the most important factor.

Discrimination and oppression

It remains only to comment upon those who are discriminated against and those who are oppressed in modern societies. All societies have major assumptions about the ways in which social roles are defined and how 'problems' are explained. Many of these assumptions are not overt, but they nevertheless bias assessments. For instance, there is a strong tendency to use the language of individual pathology to describe behaviour and attitudes which in fact have been generated by the way in which society treats some of its citizens. Methods of handling them become coercive and manipulative, reducing even further an already eroded ability on the part of these groups to participate in making decisions about their own lives. When such individuals appear united in groups, their attitudes and behaviours tend already to be stereotyped, and their obvious and apparent differences are thus wrongly ascribed and a great deal of their potential as resources is already undermined.

Differences as resources

Throughout this chapter, reference has been made to the positive side of differences – that is, that they can be resources. What are perceived as large differences infrequently become resources for the simple reason that we seem able to make use of differences only when we can see some connection or similarity, no matter how tentative, to our own position. For instance, one of the largest barriers to finding an effective solution to a problem is that all those trying to achieve a particular end are similar in many ways. In this situation, no new light is thrown onto the problem and we refer to such restricted thinking as being 'tramlined'. If someone is significantly different in some respects to the other members of a group – though not so different as to be threatening – then it is possibile that the newcomer's thinking about the group's problem will contain elements which are new and different and thus some beneficial change and progress will become possible.

However, the difference must not be too great initially, because if it is the established group members will tend to reject any proposals which stem from that difference. The main exception to this general thesis is when the newcomer has a reputation for producing workable ideas. Other than this, the main problem of using differences as resources is in finding that level of difference which, while able to produce new and different ideas, is also acceptable to the established others. Of course, the principal difficulty may lie in the refusal of group members to accept that difference has any value for them. Many groups will only accept as members those whom they can clearly assess as being similar in some essential respect to themselves.

Another problem relates to discovering and exposing difference as a resource. It is hard to break long-established habits of thinking and behaviour, particularly if they have been successful in the past, even when evidence of their inadequacy is well established. People whose habits are different because they are different and because they have had different experiences can help to change habits, to look at problems differently and to explore different ways of doing things. But their difference needs to be seen as a thing of value.

Put simply, individuals who have experienced discrimination are able to en-lighten others who have not. They may even be able to convince those who do not believe that discrimination exists in any significant way that it does. People who have had to struggle against oppressive power, whether they themselves feel they have succeeded or not, have more to offer in such a struggle than those who face it for the first time. In short, it is not just 'good' (i.e. successful) experience which is important; it is the fact that the experience is 'different' which is vital, that there are people who, whatever the quality of their experi-ence, know some of the rules of the game. Such experience has the potential to change ways of looking at things, situations and people.

Causes of failure to communicate

We have already noted that the value group members attach to what a colleague says or does is not an objective assessment of the intrinsic value of what is said or done, but is influenced to a greater or lesser extent by their perception of that individual. Thus a group member may pass on information of tremendous value to the group and find that it is almost totally ignored because the other members of the group do not like, do not trust or have a poor opinion of that member. Some years ago, the following appeared in various guises:

> I know you think you have understood what I said, but I am not so sure that what you think you have got is what I intended to convey in the first place.

This states concisely the idea that there are barriers to effective communication, some of which we will now look at very briefly.

One cause of failure to communicate is the firmly held belief that communi-cation is easy and requires little conscious effort. This may be true about very simple statements of precise fact, but as the ideas become more complex, the likelihood of any misunderstanding increases. Allied to this are socially accept-able behaviour patterns; for example, the feeling that to ask for an explanation renders one ignorant or bad mannered. This results in going along with some-thing which has not been properly understood. Subsequently, this can cause conflict due to different individuals pursuing different ends in the belief they are all pulling in the same direction.

Miscommunication also arises from the fact that individuals vary quite con-siderably in the amount of information they can absorb. Even though the infor-mation being conveyed is something the receiver could be expected to be familiar with, the rate at which he or she processes it may be very different to others equally well equipped to understand.

Another cause of failure to communicate are what are simply called 'distrac-tions'. These may be environmental in nature, such as temperature, humidity, ventilation, vibration, noise, and glare, all of which can reduce the ability of an individual to concentrate. Also, one's physical state can lead to a reduction in one's ability to concentrate. For example, when a person is suffering from a lack of sleep or is feeling unwell, has drunk too much alcohol or is on drugs (even when such drugs are prescribed and legitimate), is subject to mood changes or is under-stimulated, the ability to comprehend incoming information is drastically reduced.

The effectiveness of spoken communication can also be reduced when the message is presented against a background of other people speaking, so that it becomes increasingly difficult to shut out the extraneous or unwanted material which is being presented in the same modality (i.e. speech). Also, when individuals who are attempting to communicate with one another possess significantly different processes for dealing with information, they will find (especially if these are hidden) that references which are assumed to exist by both parties are not actually involved, so that failure of communication is almost certain. This is particularly true when it is assumed by both parties that communication has taken place: the informant thinks he or she has succeeded, and the recipient fills in the gaps from what he or she assumes to have been the gist of the message.

The information that people communicate is often confused, lacking in clarity, illogically ordered, or uses words which are ambiguous or capable of widely different interpretations. Also, people who are very similar use different constructs in their attempt to make sense of the world in which they live. Therefore, incongruities of outlook are fostered between the sexes, by membership of particular social groups, by age grouping, by social class, culture or sub-culture. Thus the very process by which messages are interpreted may be significantly different. Finally, unconscious factors like fear and anxiety, defence mechanisms, attitudes and opinions act to hinder communication, because they operate as very powerful selectors of what is actually heard and also of what interpretation is placed upon it.

Having made the point that effective communication is not the simple everyday process we believe it to be, especially when what needs to be communicated is fraught with emotion and deep feeling, then it behoves us to look at how such failure can be limited. There are four simple procedures for doing this:

1. In most cases, just asking people to tell you in their own words what they have understood you to have said will quickly reveal discrepancies. *Problems*: this process tends to run counter to acceptable social behaviour: it takes time which may not be available; and it tends to put people in an embarrassing situation.
2. Use only that form of language which is most appropriate for the situation. *Problem*: you may not know what it is.
3. When in doubt, explain, illustrate and use examples.
4. Where exact understanding is crucial, check and if possible get feedback.

> Communication is a two-way process and is thus not truly complete until some form of acknowledgement of receipt is offered by the recipient to the informant.

The differences outlined here are such that to ignore them is to reduce effective communication between the members of a group, possibly crucially. But knowing that such factors exist can mean that with some little effort group members can ensure that such failures are relatively few.

Summary of main points

This chapter presents crucial ideas about the ways in which we see others and ourselves. It asserts that we live in a world of images and interpretations of the inputs from our sensory organs, and shows how our perceptions are influenced by genetic endowment, learning, experience and environmental factors.

It also deals with the idea of 'difference' and the problems and possibilities difference causes, in particular those differences of background, culture, race, belief, power, gender and the expectations which are so important in our current society. The negative aspect of difference in terms of discrimination and oppression are discussed, resources which arise from differences which become acceptable are examined, and finally some analysis of communication is offered which shows that what we tend to accept as being a natural and efficient process of conveying information can be hindered by a number of factors which are usually ignored.

List of basic concepts and terms

Observation: the way we behave is based upon what we observe about ourselves and what we make of others and their reactions to us
Differences: both personal and socially generated; the effects they have on behaviour and on understanding.
Resources: frequently stem from difference but are the source of potential power for a group or for an individual.
Communication: considered to be natural but subject to many barriers which remain largely unknown unless conscious effort is directed to finding them.

Topics for discussion

1. Can you remember a situation in which you suddenly became aware that someone, whose opinions you respected, actually saw you in a significantly differently way to how you saw yourself? If you can, write down what you felt or thought about (a) that person, (b) yourself and (c) what, if anything, did you do about this revelation?
2. Do you consider yourself to be different to others close to you? If the answer is 'yes', (a) in what ways do you consider that difference manifests itself and

(b) what are some of the effects these differences make in your relationships with others?

3. Have you ever seriously considered how your background may have conditioned your approach to others not from the same background?

4. List those groups in society which you believe are seriously discriminated against. Then (a) describe your ideas about why such discrimination exists and (b) suggest practical ways you think it might be diminished or eradicated.

5. If one of the groups of which you are a member asked you to act as a 'resource person', what resources would you have to offer.

Reading list

Aronson, E. (1969). *The Social Animal*. W.H. Freeman and Company: San Francisco, CA. This is a general text on social behaviour, very entertainingly written but with a good use of research. For those interested in the original research articles there is a companion reader which contains all the papers in full.

Goffman, E. (1969). *Presentation of Self in Everyday Life*. Penguin Books: Harmondsworth. This is a book which presents the idea of individual behaviour being very similar to a drama i.e. a theatrical performance. It has stood the test of time and as a possible explanation of the way individuals present and think about themselves it is stimulating and provocative.

Cook, M. (ed.). (1984). *Issues in person perception*. Methuen: London and New York. This is a fairly tough text but it is well worth struggling with. It covers self understanding, how personality is perceived, the function of cues, non-verbal communication and the problems of judging the personalities of others.

Raven, B.H. and Rubin, J.Z. (1976). *Social Psychology: People in Groups*. John Wiley: New York. Chapters 2–6 are concerned with many aspects of self perception, power, self awareness, liking and disliking, all presented in a very readable way with many examples, illustrations and excerpts from research material.

Douglas, T. (1993). *A Theory of Groupwork Practice*. Macmillan: Basingstoke. This book is written around the idea that groups are most often attempts to discover and utilize the resources both current and potential which exist within a group for the benefit of the members. Chapter 4. defines what resources are and, as far as I know, this is the only text which gives such explicit information about resources.

Jones, E.E. and Nisbett, R.E. (1971). The actor and observer: divergent perceptions of the causes of behaviour. *University Programs Modular Studies*. General Learning Press: Morristown, NJ. This is a paper which presents the important differences of perception about incidents of behaviour according to whether the observer is involved in the incident or merely watching it.

7 Surviving in groups

Introduction

In order to benefit from membership of a group, it has to be maintained for a period of time. This chapter looks at how to survive in a group and covers the processes of joining, remaining a member and leaving, and the understanding and behaviours which are appropriate to successful group membership.

Groups surround us: we live, work and play in groups, and political, social, religious activities are more often than not group activities. Indeed, as we noted earlier, one of the problems of learning about groups is that groups are so common a part of our experience that the idea that there is something useful to be learned about them tends to strike us as a little strange. But while familiarity undoubtedly breeds contempt or at least indifference, it is not notorious for increasing understanding, at least not without some deliberate or conscious effort.

Thus almost without question the common level of performance in groups is much lower than it need be, because without knowledge of group processes it is seldom possible for group members to take full advantage of the resources which exist or which can be developed. When industry calls in a so-called 'trouble-shooter', what is often revealed is that familiarity has tramlined thinking and thus the opportunities which exist are not being exploited. Therefore, many people are members of work, social and leisure groups, but the costs of their membership are often higher than they need be. Survival – in this instance, meaning something better than plain existence – requires some knowledge of group process. At the very least, it requires the use of such knowledge to reduce costs and allow both the individual and the group of which he or she is a member to gain.

In Chapter 8, we will look at the specific rewards and costs which occur in group situations; here, we will look closely at those factors which have to be mastered if a solid basis for working in and with groups is to be achieved. In this respect, this chapter is also crucial in the development of understanding.

Having selected a group – one in which you are a member – and remembered the maxim that 'if you don't see something, it is not possible to do anything intentional about it', (1) how do you know what is happening in the group and (2) how do you assess in which direction, if any, it is going? Chapters 4 and 5 detail what goes on in groups and the major influences which are at work. Now it is necessary to translate this knowledge of what can exist into an ability to *see* what happens in a real group situation.

There are four areas which we can explore: (1) sensitivity, or more commonly 'gut reaction'; (2) signals, patterns and cues; (3) experience; and (4) conscious use of learned behaviour.

Sensitivity

In this context, sensitivity is a condition of increased awareness of what is going on, to be in touch with one's feelings, to be sensitized to all the indicators one has developed over the years which alert one to what is actually happening even when it is not obvious. We all have blind spots, areas where we miss the most blatant signals or which we consistently misinterpret. These blind spots we should know about because of past mistakes which have been pointed out to us. So sensitivity includes not just what we know we are aware of, but also what we have learned from experience we tend to miss or distort. Of course, if you are absorbed in a group situation, the appropriate degree of sensitivity tends to be obscured by that interest, so it is necessary to pay consciously directed attention to what your senses are picking up. An individual's sensitivity will have developed without much conscious effort, which is why it is often referred to as a 'gut reaction' (i.e. having little to do with reason or reasoning). But it is possible to check on the validity or otherwise of what the 'gut reaction' delivers over a period of time and to realize in which areas it tends to be wholly accurate and in which it is not. The more urgently one's security depends upon being sensitive to events and circumstances, the more likely it will be that one's sensitivity will display its good and bad points. It is a very important exercise in self-development to analyse past experience and to know with some certainty what are the weaknesses and strengths (see Chapter 9).

Signals, patterns and cues

These are the manifestations of incoming sensory data to some of which, in ordinary circumstances, we pay little heed. Caution needs to be exercised here because it is only by experience that the behavioural patterns of individuals come to demonstrate consistent meaning. The problem of body language, for example, is that apart from some very general and well understood signals, it is not a language at all, but a highly idiosyncratic and individual set of actions whose meaning for the performer can only be clearly ascertained by watching many repetitions. It is much more precise to know that when a given person in a group crosses his legs, this means that he finds the particular chair in which he is sitting uncomfortable than to accept a general interpretation of the movement as one which seals him off from the rest of the group.

Experience

The evaluation of your past group performances will tell you whether you pick up signals or not, whether those you picked up led you to understand their meaning correctly and eventually whether any action you took regarding them was reasonable. This implies that you need to programme your mind with information about group behaviour in general, in particular and about group members. The general data you should store and update constantly; the particular often has to be gathered afresh with each new group.

Learned behaviour

The key word here is 'conscious' and its use requires some explanation. Most of us believe that our behaviour is 'natural'. By this we mean that we pay little conscious attention to our ways of responding to people and situations unless there are special reasons for doing so, like trying to impress, or being wary because we do not know what to expect. Indeed, the idea that we 'control' our behaviour is relatively unacceptable to most people and is often regarded with some suspicion.

But if we are learning a new skill, like how to operate a computer or play a musical instrument, then conscious control of behaviour is essential, because we need to pay attention to learning what to do, when, how and in what order. In this sense, control is acceptable. But surviving in groups is a skill which has to be learned. What we already know about groups we have learned by being involved with various groups since birth, which amounts to a bag of response patterns which have helped us survive in groups – whether badly, indifferently or well. But working in groups means using the group as an instrument of care, of support, of learning, of treatment, etc. This implies that it is not just a continuation of our everyday social living which is involved, but something which is a deliberate and conscious skill applied for definite ends directed in the main at improving the quality of life for others and ourselves. So the conscious use of learned behaviour in groups is in the same category of behaviour as the conscious use of skills in any other field of human endeavour, and as such it needs to lose its connotation of being unnatural, which it appears to attract just because it is directed at human behaviour.

Let us now turn our attention to the four factors above in terms of positive survival in a group. In order to do this, I will divide the life of a group member into three: joining a group, remaining a member and leaving the group.

Group membership

There is probably as much written about newcomers to groups as there is about leadership in the literature on groups. This may be because it is one area of group experience where both group and new member are vulnerable.

In 1958, William Schutz proposed that groups have perpetually to deal with three factors, which he called inclusion, control and affection. His basic idea was that when a group is formed or when a new member joins the group, inclusion is of paramount importance to both the individual and the group as a whole. Thus a new member has to decide to what extent he or she wishes to be included in the group, and for their part the other members of the group have to decide to what extent they are prepared to include the new member in their undertakings.

Schutz suggested that over a period of time the problems relating to inclusion, for both member and group, should stabilize at a level acceptable to both parties, but by that time the next problem area would have manifested itself – the exercise of control. Once again decisions have to be made – how much control can be exercised, how much handed over and how much tolerated. Time again settles the problem of control for both group and new member, providing of course the initiate remains a member. The third factor, affection, is again established between the new member and the group as a whole over time.

Having gone through this process, Schutz indicated that a basic working relationship would then have been established, but as the group progressed towards its goals, particularly during times of crisis or significant change, the whole process of inclusion, control and affection would need to be gone through again, thus allowing the group to adjust to changing situations.

If the group was to terminate, Schutz believed that the process would have to go into reverse, so that group members would first place the affection they felt for fellow members in the context of life outside of group, then relinquish the element of control and, finally, leave the group.

It often appears as if these three factors don't follow such a neat sequence, but operate untidily at the same time and thus confuse the issue. However, this simple thesis can be represented by the following formula:

$$\text{I.C.A. [I.C.A. ...]}^n \text{ A.C.I.}$$
$$\longleftarrow \text{ Time } \longrightarrow$$

where I = inclusion factors, C = control factors, A = affection and n = the number of occurrences.

But we can introduce some important complications of this simple formula without unduly clouding its clarity, principally by including the form of group the closed form and the open form (see Table 1, point 8). It is a very different matter being a new member when all the other members are new to the group, compared with entering a group which has been established for some time. Similarly, the process is quite different when a group terminates its existence, compared with an individual leaving the group. Table 13 charts some of these differences.

Let us now look in more detail at some of the problems related to joining a group, remaining a member and leaving the group.

Joining a group

How an individual joins a group can make a considerable amount of difference to the way in which the individual and the other group members relate to one another. It might be helpful to list the ways in which entry can occur:

1. The individual is born into the group. Otherwise, individuals join groups because:
2. They choose to do so.
3. It is part of doing something else (e.g. accepting a job).
4. He or she is compelled to do so (e.g. being sent to prison).
5. He or she is compelled to do so by very specific changes in circumstances (e.g. an accident).
6. He or she drifts into it over a period of time.
7. He or she is invited to do so (e.g. join a club).
8. He or she is proud to do so (e.g. join a team).

There is some lack of distinction between these various methods of becoming a group member, but perhaps the simplest and most important factor lies in the degree of coercion which might be involved. Resentment, anger, suspicion and feeling threatened by one's entry into a group are seldom conducive to immediate and positive integration into it, though such may occur when the costs and rewards system develops a different balance, because experience illuminates satisfactions which, while they were unknown, were never part of the reckoning.

Also, some people who join groups willingly may find that what they have joined is not what they expected. Equally, those compelled by circumstances to join groups they did not choose for themselves may find that they are more attractive than originally thought. This leads to a simple statement about joining a group:

Table 13 Problems associated with group membership

	Problem	Response
1. Joining a group		
(a) New group	Wholly dependent upon knowledge and experience; no established linkages; apprehension; inability to predict	The response may be anxiety or, alternatively, brash, but essentially it initiates a process of surviving until some of the major issues involved are clearer on both sides
(b) New entrant	Apprehension, perception of possible threat; no apparent place; lack of special knowledge about the group; value and potential hidden	
2. Remaining a member	Time demonstrates some of the resources available and generates familiarity, and produces positive action. Risks are more accurately assessed – liking develops. Prediction more reliable. Work is possible as a unit. Power and security issues are settled at an acceptable level	Greater understanding of resources available; creation of an area of consensus concerned with the group's task; the beginning of a sense of belonging; increased commitment; a change in the ratio of self-interest to group interest in favour of the latter
3. Leaving the group		
(a) Group folds	Regret for ending, for issues not finished; pleasure in company and in accomplishment; a need to deal with loss (e.g. loss of support system); there is a kind of support in all doing the same thing which is not available to the individual leaving the group	Depending on success of group and the integration of new learning response, can vary from anger at termination and loss of support to sadness at the end of an enjoyable experience
(b) Individual leaving	Depletion of resources	

> It is never wise to assume that all the members of a group have joined it
> – voluntarily or not – for precisely the same reasons.

The reasons why people join a group, what they anticipate they will get out of
it and what they are prepared to commit to the group are seldom obvious, and
make a considerable difference to the way in which individuals function within
the context of the group.

Example

A young woman who was an experienced social worker was selected to
join a multidisciplinary team which had been operating for several years. The
members of the team had developed an induction process for new
members, which included written information, diagrams, graphs, statistics on
what they did, as well as time spent working alongside each member of the
team whose job it was to explain their particular role and how it fitted into
the overall process of the unit. Also included was a meeting with the team
coordinator, who demonstrated how the team fitted in with several
organizations, its administration, finance and methods of operation.

After the induction process was completed, the social worker felt she had
a good grasp of what the unit was all about. But several months later, she
was able to tell a workshop of colleagues that she was only just beginning
to realize two things: (1) that what she had been told and shown about the
group's task had been a scrupulously honest presentation of their actual
work; and (2) that although she had understood what she was being shown
and told, she had discovered that it really meant very little until she was
able to acquire some experience working with the team and to discover for
herself what the 'doing' actually was.

This example is provided for two reasons: (1) it illustrates that integration into
a group usually takes much longer than expected; and (2) it illustrates the essential
difference between information which is based upon long-term experience of its
use and the same information without the benefit of that experience.

The social worker was more than capable of understanding the information
she was being provided with during the induction period, and indeed some of
it related quite closely with her past experience. But most of it was 'understood'
in a purely rational way, and thus its meaning was quite different to the meaning
of that information for the other members of the team. When after a period of
time she had shared some of the experiences of her new colleagues, the information she had been given was seen in a different light. Indeed, she sums this
up very succinctly: 'I understood what they were telling me and I could see the
overall strategy of the unit, but now I *really know* what it involved because I am
part of it'.

So part of the process of surviving as a new member of a group is to realize that no-one can really tell you what it is like to be a member of that group. A good caring group will have a realistic expectation of the time it takes to integrate and will not push new members too hard to conform.

A common problem in this situation is that the friendliness of established members of a group to a new member can be mistaken for integration, because the new member begins to feel comfortable with his or her new colleagues. But being in a friendly relationship with colleagues is not the same thing as being an efficient functioning member. And because all groups are functioning systems which need energy and commitment from their members, it is essential that the friendliness is recognized as providing a breathing space for a new member to learn his or her place and function. Such friendliness may well continue after this learning has taken place, but it is not likely to continue if it doesn't occur, especially if the group is one in which the contributions of its members is essential to its effective functioning.

Whatever else a group may do, it undoubtedly exposes its members to each other. And herein lies a conflict that is difficult for most individuals to resolve. If a person has a strong desire or need to be accepted by a group – whether it is a comfortable conflict-free existence within the group or a desperate need for help – then this desire is accompanied by a reasoned understanding that the group will only truly accept members whose behaviour and value to the group are deemed adequate. This is often expressed as conforming to the standards of the group, being on one's 'best behaviour'. This anxiety of whether one is acceptable or not only matters if the group is important to the individual, but can be exacerbated by the fact that the rules governing acceptable behaviour in the group are not usually made explicit to the would-be entrant. Indeed, in most groups, even if a code of conduct is written down, all new members know from past experience that a considerable part of any group's conduct is governed by norms which can only be discovered by membership of the group and observing these secret rules in operation over a period of time, perhaps even coming into conflict with them.

But the other side of the conflict of being accepted concerns what groupworkers tend to call 'visibility'. In simple terms, this means that among a small group of people, particularly if they operate in each other's presence for long periods of time, individuals are essentially extremely visible to one another. Even when members of a group know one another very well, each member's behaviour is scrutinized by the others. Where familiarity is present, it is deviations from accustomed behaviour which are noticed. Where familiarity is not universally present, then all behaviour is scrutinized. In other words, this is the 'trial' period for newcomers. This has many connotations, some of which we look at here.

What are the 'factors of adaptation' which promote acceptance by the group of the new member and promote survival for that member? In its simplest form, the most effective mechanism is the search for, and exposure of, similarities (i.e. points of contact). Such points of similarity exist in virtually every aspect of human life and are just as variable in their degree of compatibility, intensity and ultimate usefulness. Thus similarity of age, appearance, occupation, gender and so on can all be called into use. But in the first instance, they must all have one thing in common – easy accessibility – which in effect means being highly visible or exposed within the compass of few words or action.

> Easily accessible points of similarity are sought by new members as their entrance to a group to reduce their sense of strangeness.

Perhaps you can remember quite clearly the feelings you experienced when leaving a job in which you were familiar with the routines and the people involved, and taking up a new post where all the knowledge you had of what to expect was secondhand and not based in personal experience. The expression 'feeling one's way' is not entirely appropriate, because individuals learn different ways of coping with the strangeness that entering a new system entails. For example, some people are brash in demonstrating to their new colleagues how experienced they are, how good and how much more important their last job was and how much they have to offer. Others are overwhelmed by the loss of support they enjoyed in their last job and, never having given much thought to how it had built up or perhaps believing that it had occurred naturally, have no idea of how to set about constructing a comfortable position for themselves in their new role.

Exercise

It is now time to think about how you coped with exactly this sort of situation in your own life. What exactly did happen? What moves did you make? How did other people help? What mistakes did you make in this process of integration? Above all, how long did it take and were your expectations realistic? Write down some answers to these questions now.

Remember that whatever information you gather about your techniques of integrating yourself into group situations, it is essentially unique to you as a person and the kind of group you were attempting to join. Nevertheless, among these patterns of behaviour you will discover certain general facts about the process of integration, so that whenever you are on the receiving end (i.e. already in a group which others want to join), remember what assisted you in your efforts and then adapt that knowledge to help the newcomers, bearing in mind that they are not you and the group may also be different in certain ways.

In the reflective exercise above lie also the seeds of an understanding about the whole process of assessment of what other people are likely to see as the kind of person you are. Sometimes the feedback you receive from these perceptions is rather surprising, because it is somewhat at odds with the mental picture you have developed of yourself. But you must remember that in the early stages of surviving in a group, the evidence possessed by the other members of the group of the kind of person you are is limited. And, like all assessments human beings make of each other, it is based upon visual appearance, rumour (if there is any), prejudice (personal likes and dislikes, which are not always logical), past experience, similarities and the individual member's ideas about what the group really needs at that moment in terms of a new member.

Over time, perceptions will change because needs will change and also because the evidence of the value of an individual will be increased by that most reliable of evidences 'demonstration'. Demonstration is something about which we need to learn a great deal. It is said that seeing is believing and in the world of group membership this is markedly true. But demonstration has to be linked with time. Let me try to explain.

You may have entered a work group, for instance, in which as part of your induction process you were told that all personal problems which might conceivably affect the quality of your work could be brought to the leader of the group for counselling and sympathetic consideration. Now there is no reason why you should doubt that this statement is a statement of true intent. But like all people who have grown up in the real world, you have learned that there is frequently a considerable discrepancy between intention and practice.

You will be most interested to see, when one of your colleagues with considerable personal problems approaches the group leader, how in fact he is received. What you will be waiting to find out is whether you will be given a demonstration at first hand of the truth of the statement or not. If the intent is clearly followed in practice, then you will no doubt feel considerably relieved and even more so when you see it happen several times to different people with different problems.

When the members of a group need to trust one another, they are dependent upon their abilities to predict the responses of their colleagues. The degree of trust there is in a given group depends to a large extent upon whether its validity has been demonstrated not once but several times. A most important survival mechanism is therefore to build up an awareness of what the group is demonstrating as its response patterns to different situations.

Remaining a member of the group

Being an effective group member and thus being a positive survivor depends upon being aware of risks, of vulnerable areas and of possible group actions which can produce a diminution of members both at a personal and unit level. There are many rewards for being an effective group member as we have seen in the matter of costs and rewards. But whereas it is customary to pay a great deal of attention to satisfaction, it is not equally customary to pay attention to risks and threats until they have produced negative results. Here we will concentrate on just two or three of the major factors of survival.

Vulnerability

In one sense, as a member of a group you are always vulnerable, but then one is at risk merely by being alive. But there are certain periods during an individual's membership of a group when that vulnerability is most pronounced and he or she is more exposed. I list these below and then discuss briefly the processes which are available to deal with them:

1. Becoming a new member (a) when the group is just forming and all the members are new, or (b) joining a group that is already in existence. Special versions of these are applicable when the new member in either case holds the position of appointed leader.
2. Member in opposition to group majority.
3. Member selected to bear the blame for group failure.
4. Member leaving group (a) when group as a whole is folding, or (b) when group continues its existence.

The major components of vulnerability are:

1. *Exposure*: a high level of visibility.
2. *Difference*: either in lack of understanding or of shared experience which is common to other members; or difference which is inherent in a given situation.
3. *Ignorance*: lack of knowledge about how to protect oneself or of what is expected.
4. *Expectation*: having learnt from experience that one usually does become a target at some stage.
5. *Personality*: this is a difficult one and should be considered with great care. It is too easy to ascribe an individual's vulnerability to a lack of social competence stemming from an inadequate personality, rather than to a lack of opportunity to learn.

Risk

A large number of people express fear of groups. This is not really surprising, because many people have had bad experiences in group situations. Even if this is not the case, they will have heard rumours of other people having such bad experiences, particularly in artificial groups. The reason I mention this is because groups can be very dangerous organizations, but usually only for those people who have either been conned into joining in some kind of group activity which they do not understand, or who have found themselves in a group and discovered that they are singularly ill-equipped either to see what is happening or to do anything about it.

Risks occur in everyday life but are mostly well known; what actually generates fear is the knowledge that unknown or different situations produce unknown risks which, because of their unforeseen nature, cannot truly be guarded against. In the most stable of groups which we inhabit, circumstances which are ordinarily well understood, make the predictability of risk, its frequency and

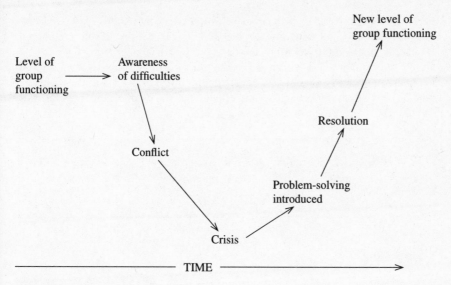

Figure 2 Levels of group functioning.

well-adapted responses almost habitual behaviour. But circumstances change and response behaviour has to change also. Thus for a period of time until circumstances restabilize, risk can increase.

It is of great interest to those who endeavour to help others learn about groups, how unquestioning learners can be. They appear able to place unlimited faith in people if they believe them to possess superior knowledge and skill, even though they have no real evidence that these assumptions are accurate. It becomes axiomatic that entrants into any new group, particularly a group that purports to have as its basic aim learning about groups, should not accept on trust what they do not understand. All effective group training situations have certain well-defined areas of learning (sometimes experiential), but none which are more effective for being hidden or for demanding implicit trust without understanding. So ask! And if this means that you are regarded as a nuisance or even thrown out of the group, then you may be quite sure that had you stayed, the outcome may well have been very painful but of little intrinsic value.

> No group learning situation which is basically dependent upon deception by the trainer of the learner has much of value to offer.

There is another risk factor worth mentioning, which concerns the matter of offered choice. It must be borne in mind that when an individual is offered a choice, but has no understanding of the alternatives offered or of their respective merits, it is not a true choice, no matter how much it may look like one. Choice occurs, in the true sense, between a selection of known alternatives when the relevant data and understanding are available to the person making the choice. Of course, some choices have to be made on the basis of minimal data, for the simple reason that that is all there is. Often in such circumstances, choices may be modified later when more data are available. But it is axiomatic about choices that they are always only as good and effective as the evidence upon which they are based.

A good and effective choice is one that is based on adequate information and which is understood by the person making the choice in his or her own terms.

Scapegoating

Scapegoating is a survival procedure, but not for individuals. It is a process which is implemented to preserve the group. As far as group members are concerned, it is necessary for their survival prospects for them to be aware of how the process operates, but most importantly how scapegoats appear to be selected.

The process is one of transferring blame. Thus when a group feels that it is not making progress or that it is producing a lot of bad feelings, anger, distrust or resentment, it needs some way of discharging these bad feelings without destroying the group. Confrontation, unless in circumstances which are secure enough to contain such an emotional discharge, can be immensely destructive and is thus to be used with caution.

The method usually employed ('chosen' is not the right word to use, as the process seems to arise without apparent conscious effort on the part of members) is that of blaming particular members of the group for what is happening. When blame is attached to a person, a considerable degree of relief is felt by all the other members of the group, even though they know that the victim is no more to blame than they are. The process is found in all walks of life and seems to be one of the more stable processes of evading responsibility and for the transfer of blame.

But scapegoats do not appear to be chosen at random. They tend to be selected on the basis that they display some very obvious difference. Also, scapegoats are often volunteers. The following are the sorts of member used as scapegoats:

1. Group members with no great ability to retaliate when attacked and are seen as possessing little social power (though sometimes when it is the leader who is chosen, they are seen as having too much).
2. Those who possess easily recognized personal characteristics which promote dislike (e.g. Odd appearance, provocative behaviour, etc.).

3. Those who offer themselves for attack and actually appear to expect and provoke it – they complain of being put upon.
4. Those who appear to be dragging their feet and impeding the group's progress towards its goals.

Scapegoating tends to be used more frequently when the group's cohesion is weak, as for instance when it is moving from one stage to another and the new situation is not yet fully consolidated. But however it occurs, its main function is to save the group, thus gaining time to consider its position. Usually, whoever is selected is regarded as expendable, though the main difference between the classical religious version of the scapegoat and the group version is that the latter is not usually driven from the group but pushed to the periphery, ready to be used again should the need arise. This being so, wherever some attempt is being made in a group to prevent scapegoats being used, it is well to remember that some other form of dealing with the group's bad feelings needs to be substituted.

Finally, it must be noted that prejudice, dislike and hostility towards given individuals within the group are frequently used as the basis for choosing a scapegoat. As these factors often change during the life of a group, different individuals may be chosen to be the scapegoat, but some people may fulfil the role more or less permanently.

Being involved in the decision-making process

One well-established fact about groups is that when all the members of a group are involved in the decision-making process and perceive themselves to be an integral and involved part of that process, they tend to believe in any decisions made and it becomes very difficult to change them. Thus to be an active group member is to take part in any discussion of group action.

When members are excluded from participation in decision-making, then they offer less commitment to such decisions and may indeed oppose them or sabotage them. A working definition of helplessness and powerlessness in groups can be based on the idea of members knowing that decisions which affect major areas of their lives were made by others and that they were excluded from participation and consultation.

Members who do not take part in decision-making are thus pushed to the periphery of the group's power structure and their costs are increased and their rewards diminished. If there are alternatives available when this balance becomes critical, they may well leave. If there are no available escape routes, then they will remain as time-serving members with considerable loss to the group in terms of wasted resources.

Peripheral members are those members whose survival in the group is uncertain. Indeed, one of the reasons for such people being chosen as scapegoats is that the remaining members of the group see them as a handicap to progress and may even regard them as superfluous to the best interests of the group.

Table 14 The characteristics of self-selecting victims and techniques for dealing with scapegoating

---

The characteristics of self-selecting victims:
1. An inability to deal with the aggression of others
2. A strong tendency to be passive
3. An inability to cope with one's own angry feelings
4. Probably having strong feelings of guilt
5. An expectation of being rejected, ridiculed or punished
6. May be confused about gender role
7. May produce excessive attention-seeking behaviour
8. Poorly organized or weak aggressive drive
9. Is visibly different in some obvious way
10. Demonstrates a marked ambivalence to those of high standing within the group

Such a person:
1. Repeatedly puts him or herself in contact with persons and situations which are injurious to him or her as defined on past experience
2. Appears to show no evidence of learning from experience in this situation
3. Shows a marked tendency to exacerbate potentially dangerous situations
4. Provokes, is attacked and attacks back, and then points to his or her being attacked as the reason for his or her retaliation
5. Seems to deny consistently that there is any pattern of persecution or that it is sought
6. Also seems continuously to assert that the situation is bad but beyond his or her control

Techniques which have been advocated for dealing with scapegoating:
1. Squash the scapegoating behaviour
2. Select group members carefully to avoid possible victims
3. Bring out into the open the processes of scapegoating
4. Operate to protect the victim by stronger members
5. Create a diversion
6. Reduce the level of interaction between members
7. Attempt to strengthen the scapegoated member
8. Work with the group as a whole to clarify the process of scapegoating
9. Focus the group's activities and attention on dealing with the problem
10. Encourage the group to exercise control over the process
11. Role-play the situation to generate understanding
12. Remove the scapegoats from the group

Leaving a group

As when joining a group, the manner of leaving also has differential consequences for the individual and the group. Here is a list of the possible ways of
leaving:

1. When the group as a whole comes to an end:
    (a) because it has run its course; or
    (b) because it falls apart.
2. When members leave an ongoing group:
    (a) because they have achieved all or most of what they joined for;
    (b) because they have not achieved what they wanted;
    (c) because they have found alternatives which appear more rewarding;
    (d) because they are compelled to leave by outside circumstances; or
    (e) because they are evicted by the group.

All of these have consequences for both the group – in those situations where
the group continues to exist – and for the individuals who leave, most of which
are reasonably obvious in terms of satisfaction or not. Here we look at just two
areas: loss and consolidation.

Loss

Both the group and the member leaving will experience loss. In the first instance, the loss is primarily concerned with resources, but it also concerns relationships, friendship ties and ultimately numbers. This, however, is often ignored,
despite the fact that the number of people in a group may be a very important
factor (e.g. for the weight of opinion in discussions, etc.).

Consolidation

When an individual leaves a group, either because the group folds or because
the individual him or herself departs, some consolidation of the learning to be
obtained from the experience is essential. In this context, consolidation means
that whatever learning or change took place within the group which was of value
to the individual member, becomes integrated into that individual, thus helping
him or her to survive when the group is no longer there to reinforce it. This
means that consolidation is not just something that happens after a member
leaves a group, but should have been part of the process throughout his or her
membership.

Support

As we have seen, leaving a group entails loss and one of the major areas of loss
is in the matter of support. It is often relatively easy to maintain and utilize new
attitudes, new learning and new insights within the supportive framework of the

group which helped to create them. It is an entirely different matter to sustain such new development in a relatively unsupportive and uncaring outside world. So consolidation should start in the supportive group with a preparation process that highlights methods of coping with the withdrawal of group support. While this is very important in groups which are specifically designed to support and change their members, it is also important where the main objectives are social or educational. The compassionate quality of such groups meets some very essential human needs and there is some requirement to prepare for loss of belonging and support. Perhaps the most important survival strategy here is that the transition from group member to non-group individual should be recognized as a process of change, and while not exaggerating the consequences of such a change to ensure that awareness exists of the possibility of loss.

Finally positive survival is wholly dependent upon understanding the group as a system, with its costs and rewards, and in being able thus to make rational and logical choices of available options.

> The ability to choose rather than to be unaware that choice exists is a prime element in being a responsible individual.

Summary of main points

Primarily, this chapter has dealt with the need to see what is going on in a group by translating knowledge of group processes into a pragmatic sensitivity to the cues and patterns of behaviour which occur in groups. The process of surviving in a group has been discussed in relation to actually becoming a member; to remaining in a group and actively pursuing a membership role; and, finally, to leaving a group both when the group remains and also when it does not. It has been stressed that effective involvement in group processes means being suffi- ciently aware of them to be able to direct commitment in the most appropriate ways.

List of basic concepts and terms

Observation: seeing what goes on, but involves more than just looking.
Inclusion: joining a group and deciding on the level of integration which is appropriate.
Control: the degree of influence and power which a member is prepared both to accept from others and exert him or herself.
Affection: the degree of mutual liking between members.
Similarity: often used as an early linking technique by new members.

Self-image: because of the high visibility which exists within a group, there is a need for each member to be reasonably aware of how they appear to others.
Remaining a member: usually depends upon the level of satisfaction achieved by the group and members with each other.
Vulnerability and risk: visibility in a group exposes members; the development of trust based largely on predictability reduces the force of being at risk.
Choice: real choice is dependent upon the individual making the choice really understanding what is on offer.

Topics for discussion

1. Write down the process as you remember it of being admitted to a group and if possible the process of leaving it.
2. What do you understand by being 'inducted' into a group? List what you think are the main aims of such a process.
3. Why does the process of leaving a group often entail a sense of loss? Can you relate these ideas to the proliferation of reunions in some forms of social groups and to other forms of keeping in contact?
4. Why do you think staying in a group is referred to here as 'surviving'.

Reading list

Raven, B.H. and Rubin, J.Z. (1976). *Social Psychology: People in Groups*. John Wiley: New York. Although a general social psychology text, the authors cover many useful topics of group behaviour in Chapters 8–10, in particular how groups can affect the performance of individuals, what group norms and judgements are, decision-making and leadership processes, etc. It must be remembered that a book such as this is research-oriented and there are no specific attempts to relate any findings to practical experience except in a very general sense. Thus it is necessary to make some attempt to translate the generalities to accommodate a particular viewpoint (i.e. that of being a group member). This is not difficult, because the text is both entertaining and well written.

Tajfel, H. and Fraser, C. (1978). *Introducing Social Psychology*. Penguin: Harmondsworth. In the second part of this text, the authors cover interpersonal behaviour, communication, cooperation and competition, all from a non-specific viewpoint. Chapters 7 and 8 are about groups and contain some ideas relevant to survival as a group member. But once again these ideas need to be translated from unbiased observer or researcher viewpoint to that of group member.

8 The rewards, costs and dangers of group membership

Introduction

What are rewards and costs? Some indication of what these might be was provided in the last chapter in terms of vulnerability and risks. This chapter explores the following rewards which result from group membership: companionship; the possibility of learning about oneself, of gaining in experience and developing a sense of belonging; gaining access to resources, help with problems and difficulties; gaining an increased understanding of how groups function; and what chances there are for bringing about change. In the costs section we deal with stultification, bad habits, stress, reductions in social contact, prejudice, attack, exploitation, loss of choice and rejection.

In his play *Lady Windermere's Fan*, Oscar Wilde defined a cynic as 'A man who knows the price of everything and the value of nothing'. But one does not have to be a cynic to know that all actions that human beings take entail consequences which can be seen in terms of costs or rewards. Economists, for instance, are fond of describing 'economic man', by which they mean an individual who makes choices about how he will dispose of his available income. Such choices entail consequences. For example, by choosing to have a particular item, economic man reduces or precludes the possibility of having something else. Thus one of the costs of choosing the first item is the necessity of having to forego others. Whereas in economic terms such choices entail relatively clear consequences and costs, in social behaviour terms the consequences and costs of choices are not so clear.

Let us take the simple example of an individual joining a choir. The choir is a group which makes demands upon its members, usually in terms of requiring their physical presence on a regular basis over a period of time, a degree of commitment to learn, to practise, to perform, etc. The rewards are reasonably obvious – enjoyment in the exercise of musical ability, the sense of being a creative member of a team, the pleasure of associating with people of like interests, and so on. But what are the costs? There is the amount of time the individual has to commit to the choir, the need to travel to venues and the fact that the individual is unable to do other things and be with other people during the time spent with the choir.

These may well be costs which the individual is quite prepared to pay, as he or she is gaining more satisfaction from being a member of the choir than if he or she were not. However, the consequences for other people may not be so positive. How often do we hear of individuals devoting so much time and energy to a particular aspect of their life because they derive great satisfaction from it, that others around them suffer the unforeseen costs of reduced satisfaction?

We have therefore to be aware that there is a strong tendency for the major social consequences entailed by social behaviour, particularly if change is involved, to be those which were not anticipated when the original movement to change was initiated.

This leads onto the concept of reward or satisfaction. If we have the choice, we are likely to leave a social situation in which the costs of remaining in it are greater than the rewards. Note that I am careful to suggest that this would occur *if we had the choice*. In a number of group situations, such a choice is not available and the consequences of that need to be considered very carefully.

It is not possible to leave certain groups because of their confining nature; for example, it is not possible for a prisoner to terminate his or her membership of the prison population. However, the group in question might also function in everyday life. For example, a family unit may have to remain in a given locality because they are unable to sell their house; or an individual may be constrained by his job due to his terms of employment. Many people find themselves in such a situation some time during their life. The phrase 'make the best of a bad job' is apt here, but to do so is frequently much more difficult than we realize.

Responses to finding oneself trapped in a group situation vary from straight-forward rebellion to withdrawal of commitment, except that which is basic and necessary to survive, and where possible to seek a counterbalancing satisfaction from some source other than the group itself. If you work with people in a group whose situation is like this, you must be aware that this will be a weak group in terms of the level of commitment to it by most of its members. Thus any attempt to induce such a group to work must be related specifically and clearly to producing an increase in satisfaction for those involved.

This simple statement is fraught with hidden difficulties, not least in discov-ering what would actually constitute increased satisfaction for the group mem-bers involved. Far too often what constitutes satisfaction is decided by people whose real knowledge of the quality of life of the group members is wholly external to the group and thus unlikely to be relevant. For example, attempts in one residential home to control the behaviour of resident groups by rewarding acceptable behaviour with privileges were not very successful, because the resi-dents believed that the privileges on offer were theirs by right and had been taken away from them when they first entered the residential home. The reward value of such privileges were thus minimal. Any reward has to be perceived as such by the person being rewarded, not merely a reinstatement of something previously withdrawn (unless its withdrawal was part of a deliberate and under-stood plan). A major problem of defining what a reward actually constitutes, is the idiosyncratic nature of individuals – something which is perceived by one person as a reward will not be by another.

Social workers and others are frequently confronted by an apparent inability on the part of their clients to make changes in lifestyle and behaviour which are considered well within their range. Why? Are the perceived costs in terms of the effort required too great? Is complaining about their situation a sufficient release of frustration to make change unnecessary? Are there other satisfactions hidden within the situation which are highly individual and not available for outside consideration? The fact that no clear-cut answer is readily available should not deter us from attempting to discover what the costs and rewards of group membership might be supposed to be. One simple reason should suffice. All group membership invites some degree of conflict between two forms of commitment, commitment to the group and commitment to oneself. As all groups are energy systems, and as the energy source is simply the commitment of members to the group, then the relationship between commitment to the group and commitment to self or other is extremely important for the health and unity of the group.

One further point. Some groups require little commitment on the part of their members to allow them to function efficiently. Others cannot function at all unless that commitment is very strong and durable. Thus the level of commitment to a group is not only related to the willingness of members to give it, but also to the degree of energy which is appropriate to the function of the group in question. It is as possible for members to destroy a group by committing an inappropriately

Table 15   Rewards available to group members

1. Companionship, reduced isolation, the provision of social networks to help establish and maintain one's identity
2. The possibility of learning about oneself and the way others respond to us; updating one's self-image
3. Experience of working with others to generate benefits for all
4. Belonging – the development of a sense of being wanted by others and of being useful; a climate of warmth
5. Access to resources which as individuals we do not possess
6. Help with, and diminution of, problems and difficulties, often from people of similar but distinct experience and thus with high credibility
7. Increased understanding of the ways in which groups can and do influence human behaviour
8. The chance of effecting personal change in a supportive environment

large amount of energy to it as it is to cause it to wither away by not offering enough commitment.

A word of caution is advisable at this point. The title of this chapter would seem to suggest that human groups produce what might be called standard benefits and inevitable losses for members. Now whereas this is in part true, it needs some qualification. It must be stressed that the nature and quality of both benefits and disadvantages are conditioned by the circumstances operating in particular group, and what in some groups may be a distinct advantage may constitute a disadvantage in others. For instance, to be a member of a group which cares deeply about its members can be a wonderful experience for those individuals who have been isolated and uncared for, but for members who require challenge and conflict to bring the best out of them, such a group could be stifling and hence unproductive. So when we come to consider the major benefits and losses which can arise for the individual and the group, it is well to bear in mind that circumstances can make a considerable difference to the quality of the factors we are considering.

However, on a positive note, let us start by considering the major rewards available for group members (see Table 15).

Analysis of rewards

Becoming a group member

It has been said that a group actually becomes a recognizable entity in its own right when the individuals of which it is composed become 'members'. Now this is an intriguing concept, because it seems to imply that acquiring membership means entering into a new and different state. But as we have seen, we are members of groups all our lives, and whereas it is quite viable to state that

Table 16 Factors that increase and decrease the attractiveness of a group

Increased attractiveness	Decreased attractiveness
1. The prestige a group is seen to have	1. Disagreements among members
2. The setting in which a group operates	2. Excessive or unreasonable demands made by the group on its members
3. The amount of interaction between its members	3. Dominating or unpleasant behaviours
4. The relevance of its size	4. Much self-oriented behaviour
5. The perception that it is a successful group	5. Limitation on activities imposed by the group
6. The qualities of its members	6. Negative evaluation of membership by outsiders
	7. Much inter-group competition
	8. The existence of more attractive alternatives

membership of these groups conveys some distinction (e.g. in a family it confers a definite set of relationships with others according to their place in the family hierarchy; in a business organization another and different set of relationships is based on the hierarchical structure of the organization), does it mean anything worth considering?

Both the examples given above concern group organizations which tend to be accepted as 'natural' groups, in the sense that they have existed for a long time in human society, are accepted and are regarded as having long traditions. But when we come to consider groups which are usually described somewhat disparagingly as 'artificial' (i.e. groups which have no long tradition of value to society and which are deliberately and consciously created for specific ends), is the picture somewhat different?

Individuals become members of 'created' groups (i.e. those whose main reason for existence is to use the influences which operate within them for specific and chosen ends) either out of choice, that is voluntarily, or after some degree of coercion by others, usually on the basis that the individual's membership will prove beneficial.

Almost everyone will find him or herself the member of a number of different groups – both large and small – for a variety of reasons. Tables 16 and 17 help to illustrate (1) those factors about a group which make it attractive to actual and potential members, (2) those factors which serve to reduce a group's attractiveness and (3) what consequences increased attractiveness of a group may have.

Learning about oneself

One of the most effective ways of learning something about oneself is to receive and monitor responses from others in a situation which offers support and a degree of understanding. Reference has already been made to 'blind spots', kinds of behaviour produced by individuals in response to certain situations in which they find themselves but of which they are not aware of having produced. Such responses may well have been consciously learned at an earlier stage of

Table 17   The consequences of a group being attractive

1. Members are more inclined to accept responsibility
2. Attendance is likely to be better
3. The level of participation will be higher
4. Members will not give up their efforts easily
5. Members will be open to interpersonal influence
6. Members will be more willing to listen to others
7. Members will be more flexible in accepting pressure
8. Members will make more attempts to influence others
9. Members will adhere to the standards of the group and will exert pressure on others to do likewise
10. Members will tend to experience enhanced well-being

development and for a considerable period have served a useful purpose. But as the number of their usages multiplied, they became what is commonly known as 'knee-jerk' responses (i.e. they appear without conscious intent or purpose).

It is self-evident that such behavioural patterns will elicit responses in those at whom they are directed and that these responses may well seem somewhat peculiar to the individual producing the 'blind' behaviour because he or she is unaware of what they have done. This therefore provides ample scope for misunderstanding, as an interpretation of responses has to be provided and in this case will frequently be founded on very shaky ground. In all types of human relationships, a universal and important recipe for disaster stems from inaccurate interpretations of signals, which once set in motion tends to spiral out of control until a state of confrontation exists.

Not all groups are equally effective in providing feedback to members. Indeed, some groups are bound by strict rules which, when followed, tend to eliminate behaviour that would elicit comment. For this reason, any reward should be seen as a possibility rather than a certainty. However, at least small groups offer members the possibility of learning if one is accepted or not, even if the feedback is not in the form of direct comment and it is only the supremely self-satisfied or the abysmally ignorant who feel that they have nothing to learn about themselves from contact with others.

Finally, I do not wish to suggest that learning new things about oneself implies that change, when what is disclosed is unsatisfactory, should be instigated. But what *is* implied is that such knowledge introduces the possibility of change if it is thought necessary, a possibility which was previously unavailable. All that these insights actually demand is that an increased awareness of blind spots should make it possible to allow for their effects and thus possibly reduce the incidence of poor interpretations of received responses.

Division of labour

One way of dealing with complex tasks or problems is to break them down into their component parts and deal with them separately. Economists tend to call this process the 'division of labour'. It implies that in a particular community, however large or small, that instead of undertaking many different tasks, individuals do a single or far fewer jobs for the community as a whole or, alternatively, work as part of a larger project. In modern society, we are so dependent on others providing many of the necessities of life that if we did have to do things for ourselves, most of us would not survive for long because we no longer have the requisite knowledge or skills.

Specialization is now seen as part of the fabric of everyday life and we accept dependence upon others as normal, a fact which makes the withdrawal of labour such a profoundly disturbing weapon in industrial disputes, which depends to some extent upon the degree of dependence which large sections of the community place upon the services withdrawn. But a certain change in thinking regarding the division of labour has to be made when we come to look at how it is applied within some kinds of groups. So let us try to clarify the distinctions:

1. *Specialization*: a process by which an individual or small group performs one of many tasks that need to be done, but doing it for the community as a whole and receiving in return the services performed by other individuals or small groups.
2. *Breakdown*: this occurs when a large or complex project is broken down into its component parts, which are then allocated as tasks to individuals or small groups in the community. Ultimately, all the individuals and small groups will combine their efforts to complete the project or solve the problem.

These divisions are related to a specific task or problem. But groups which have support or change of their members as their basic objective seem to employ a different version of division, in that what is divided seems not to be a task but experience.

Example

A group of people recently discharged from psychiatric care was formed by mental health social workers. The avowed purpose of the group was two-fold: (1) to provide a forum for discussion of the problems involved in a return to the community and (2) for the social workers to offer support in the form of information and direct action on request. The reports of the workers involved showed that not only was the group successful, in that many discharged patients were referred to it, but also that the most effective support and that which was most in demand was promoted by the members themselves for each other.

The form of division of labour in this group was made possible because each member had access to the wide range of credible experience on offer. One major problem for those who seek to offer wider personal experience is that often those who possess it do not regard it as valuable, either for themselves or for others. The recognition of its worth only occurs when they are free to compare what they have with the experience of others and to see difference and similarity.

One final point about the division of labour in this last sense is that it is dependent upon the perception of the individuals involved of the credibility of others. Take the following scenario between helpers and clients:

Client: And what can you do to help me?

Worker: Well I have worked with many people in your situation and have been able to help sort out problems of accommodation and finance and so on.

Client: Oh yes – and what about them? [pointing to the group she had expressed some reluctance to join].

Worker: They all have similar difficulties to the ones you're trying to deal with at the moment.

Client: So if they need help themselves, how are they going to be able to help me?

Some weeks later, the same client is now a member of the group:

Worker: Do you remember saying 'how are this lot going to help me when they need help themselves?'

[Laughter in the group]

Client: [slightly embarrassed] . . . Yeah, well – they know what it's all about – they've been in it haven't they? They know what the real problems are. Not like you lot!

[More laughter at social worker's expense]

Worker: [with good humour] . . . So you think they've helped?

Client: Of course they have – I've got more understanding from them about being, you know, depressed, than I ever got from doctors and such!

Finding a place

For many people, membership of a group means that for at least a part of their lives they are part of a network of relationships which has some element of familiarity about it and which generates a sense of belonging. It does not have to be a very strong or important relationship to be effective, depending on what the actual purpose of the group and of being a member is. In weak groups, the attachment may be quite loose, but at least it exists and it tends to define boundaries for individual members. In strong groups, the attachment, the rewards and the demands will be much greater, and it is possible to see how such groups are inclusive, how they bind together and support their members. But they are also exclusive, in that they keep other individuals out by denying them membership. Strong groups have very clear boundaries and the difference between 'them' and 'us' is very distinct, and is emphasized and encouraged. Often intense loyalty marks the members of a strong group and there is usually pride in the group and in its achievements. Members take great pains to make known the difference between their group and others which might be in the same line of business.

Access to resources

Perhaps the most obvious and instant advantage of membership of any group is that it offers access to resources otherwise not available. Even if the group is a weak unit, in the sense that its component members work in close physical proximity to one another but are not dependent upon one another for the performance of the group task. In such a group, some members may be relatively new and inexperienced, whereas others will have been members for a long time and have experience to offer. Sub-groups will also exist, based on friendship or some other shared characteristic. There will also be a sense of belonging, however weak and unaffectionate it may be.

A large number of groups are created in order to exploit the increased resources which become available to group members. Resources in this context are everything of value which human beings possess or to which they have access. Thus they range from the kind of person an individual may be (e.g. having an ability to understand, to be sympathetic, kind, etc.) to knowledge and experience, skills, memories, information, contacts, etc. The more intimate and personal the resources a group needs, the greater the trust they need to develop in each other.

One of the most exciting things about resources is the different values they possess for different people. For instance, in a staff group which had been set up to design a long-term programme for dealing with the transfer of the mentally ill from hospital to community care, the most recent member in the group was also the one with by far the least experience of work of this nature. He was very impressed by his colleagues' experience, but over time he became aware that their planning skills were of a low order. Very hesitantly he suggested ways of improving aspects of the plan under consideration. Eventually, it dawned on his colleagues that maybe here were skills which they did not possess. He modestly assured them that everybody knew what he knew, but as it turned out he had learnt computer programming and was able to write a program for the department's problems in a very short time. He regarded such an ability as commonplace and of very little account. But in the context of the staff problem, it was a scarce and valuable resource.

It is often the case that what individual members of a group regard either as a failure to cope or as a very limited and inadequate survival programme, contains ideas and attitudes, information and help for others in a similar position, most of which had never previously occurred to them. The fact that people survive catastrophes and crises may indicate that however poorly they think they have performed, there must have been some successful elements in what they did. Indeed, the lack of success as seen by the individual is often actually occasioned by comparing what was achieved to some abstract standard which it is believed, should have been attained.

A group is a resource system and resources are what individual members bring with them to the group plus those they develop during their membership. There are a number of problems associated with locating and using resources, and we will consider these later.

Help with problems

'Two heads are better than one' is a common saying which has a large element of wisdom in it. Western society lays great stress on individuality, which has been responsible for obscuring group influence but more importantly for making individuals feel they are failures if they are unable to run their lives successfully within the scope of their own resources. One response to this situation has been the rise of specialists, because it is acceptable to use professionals to help plug deficiencies in personal resources. Such is the complexity of life that no one individual is deemed to possess sufficient resources to cope with all the eventualities of his or her life.

Obviously, when the knowledge and skill required is of a very high order, then specialists are essential; but many of the problems we face are matters of coping with everyday existence and the subsequent changes in circumstances. What is required here is practical wisdom. But the problem of using practical wisdom has always been its idiosyncratic nature. Thus if A offers help to B, the help will tend to be based upon A's experience of coping with a similar situation to that of B, but will be specifically related to the kind of person A is, his perception of the problem, his resources and his personality, all of which may be not particularly applicable to B who is after all a different person. But in the context of a group, there would be a variety of responses from different individuals to B's problem, offering a spectrum of help within which and across which it would be more likely that B would find something of use. This spread of available information and experience also has credibility in that it visibly comes from people who are relating personal experience – that is, first-hand experience – which can overcome the weakness of this kind of resource when it comes from a single person.

Group help has another advantage, in that it tends to be offered in a form of words and behaviour which is more likely to be compatible with the individual understanding of the group member at whom it is aimed than if it were to come from a specialist. This is not to decry specialists, who usually have a much wider grasp of the problems in their subject area.

Group help also tends to reduce an individual's sense of isolation and of personal inadequacy through the very rewarding process of familiarity.

Understanding how groups work

As this book is devoted to the idea that an increase in the understanding of how groups work is a change for the better, I need not comment extensively on this form of reward. Perhaps it will suffice to say that learning about how groups work will not only benefit the individual in the workplace, but also in many other aspects of living where groups exist. Once a basic understanding of group functioning has been grasped, then the dynamics of committees, friendship groups and families can be revealed for what they actually are. However, the closer and more emotionally involved an individual is with a particular group, the harder it is to see past that involvement to the mechanics of the group situation. But there are ways in which such observations can be improved.

As we have already noted, it is much easier and simpler to see the consequences of behaviour in groups than to attribute reasons for the behaviour, which are often hidden. The effects behaviour produces when visible are what are known as the group processes. Thus to ask what happened, who set it in motion, what the outcomes are, who gains and who loses, is to look for answers which involve visible processes and which, deriving from individual motivation, are much more readily observable.

Example

A group was discussing ways of solving its financial crisis. Many ideas were put forward, each of which seemed to be flawed. Then an idea was proposed which seemed to fit the bill, but one long-standing member began to argue against the idea. Because he was a powerful and much respected member, his arguments were listened to with care and indeed he was beginning to persuade the other group members to reject the idea. Then another member who had said little but had watched very carefully entered the argument. Indirectly, as if he was not quite sure of his facts, he was able to show that the negative arguments were not really valid and were based not upon the value of the proposal but upon a personal antipathy the long-standing member had for the proposer dating from a quarrel some time previously. This was an example of an individual attempting to use the group to settle a personal score and being prevented by another who used his understanding of group dynamics to expose what was happening.

Support

Individuals choose to join groups which support them by apparently reinforcing views and beliefs which they already hold, by offering to increase the amount of appropriate information which is available to them and by offering standards against which they can compare themselves. In many cases, the support stems from the perceived credibility of members arising from similar shared life experiences and the perception of there being a similar outlook and understanding which is practical in its origin and not theoretical. In such supportive surroundings, many group members experience a sense of security and safety and a diminution of alienation, isolation and difference, which can constitute a considerable reward.

Analysis of costs

Table 18 lists some of the more common costs associated with group membership. Any process which produces rewards can, if put into reverse or even withheld, introduce costs. For instance, those influences which can generate

Table 18   The possible costs of group membership

1. Stultification	A group can reduce all its members to a common level of performance, thus restricting and confining those who are different or more capable, creating frustration and possibly apathy, rebellion or withdrawal
2. Bad habits	The very process of conformity may make members accept bad or asocial behaviour as easily as acceptable behaviour
3. Stress	Groups can expect too much from their members, thereby increasing anxiety, especially if the costs of opting out are also high
4. Reducing social contact	Essentially, time spent in one group entails not spending it somewhere else; but the cohesion of some groups precludes members being part of other groups
5. Prejudice	Because groups affirm and support particular beliefs and viewpoints, the possibility of reinforcing prejudice is quite strong
6. Attack	Some members can become the repository of bad feelings within a group, especially if they are seen as significantly different from other members or as delaying progress (see section on scapegoats on p. 110)
7. Exploitation	Members' loyalty and need for acceptance can be exploited by stronger and more powerful members
8. Loss of possible alternatives	If membership does not produce the ends expected, then the loss is exacerbated if available alternatives existed at the time of joining which subsequently prove to have been a better bet
9. Rejection	Members are evicted from the group, ignored, mocked or pushed to the periphery

changes in behaviour and which are regarded as not only personally rewarding but also socially adaptive can, if applied in different areas and directions, produce change which may be rewarding to the individual but socially unacceptable. One of the arguments against locking up persistent juvenile offenders is that secure units have as much chance of becoming training schools of crime as they have of becoming rehabilitation units.

Stress within groups may be due to a number of causes. For example, too much may be expected of members, but group members may also be the focus of group attention which, while it may not be hostile, may be something which some individuals find very difficult to cope with.

As the idea of the costs of group membership are often the negative images of rewards, I think Table 18 is sufficiently self-explanatory not to need further elaboration, except to add one final point. The need of some group members to remain members of a particular group may be so great that they will tolerate what appears to be an enormous burden of cost.

Table 19   Factors which deter groups from working effectively

1. Disagreement about ways to deal with issues
2. Unreasonable or excessive demands made by the group
3. Dominating or unpleasant members
4. A high degree of self-oriented behaviour
5. The group in some way is seen to be limiting the 'outside' satisfactions of its members
6. The negative assessment of the value of membership made by significant people outside of the group
7. Overt competition with other groups unless the group is in a winning position
8. Other groups exist that are better able to meet the needs of members

Example

One young male member of a group of patients recently discharged from a psychiatric unit was apparently unable to control his sense of fun, whereas his peers were rather serious about their problems. Week after week this young man was subjected to ridicule, anger and abuse by the other group members in an effort to get through to him that his behaviour was not acceptable. Yet week after week he turned up and suffered the indignities heaped on him by his fellow members. When asked why he continued to attend group meetings, his reply was quite sobering. He found the apparently intolerable situation of the group infinitely more satisfying to the isolation and loneliness he would otherwise experience. For two hours each week he had succeeded in the only way he could of being the centre of attention.

What appears inexplicable tolerance of a situation to some people may actually be a reward to others when seen in relation to the rest of their lives.

One considerable cost to members occurs when the group fails to function, for in essence this means that their commitment to the group begins to look like a waste of time and effort, which could have been better devoted elsewhere.

Costs and rewards are often very personal in nature, so it is well to consider that apparently inexplicable behaviour may be a response to quite hidden factors. This becomes a serious problem when termination of group membership is not possible. When the costs to an individual of remaining a member of a group are high and there is no way of terminating membership, then withdrawal, anger, violent behaviour and apathy become the real options, indeed the only ones available.

Summary of main points

In essence, the rewards an individual receives for becoming and remaining a group member are difficult to assess in some cases. But as long as they outweigh any costs involved, the individual will usually find that particular situation satisfying. If the costs outweigh any current or future rewards, then that individual will attempt to terminate his group membership. If termination of group membership is not an option, then non-cooperative behaviour, withdrawal, anger or apathy may well be seen. What constitutes rewards or costs for an individual can usually only be hinted at by the behaviour of that individual (e.g. remaining in a social situation which would seem to others to be intolerable). This is only possible if there are hidden and intensely personal rewards for that individual.

List of basic concepts and terms

Groups only exist if their members stay together for some period of time.
Group attractiveness: a group is attractive to its members when it provides an excess of satisfactions (rewards) over dissatisfactions (costs).
Resources: these are all those facilities which become available to a group member which he or she did not possess before or was unable to use, including knowledge, ideas, behaviour patterns, etc.

Topics for discussion

1. Take any group of which you have been a member for some time and draw up a balance sheet of costs and benefits. List what you consider to be the merits and drawbacks of membership. What is the balance of the account?
2. If the costs outweigh the rewards, are you still a member of the group? If you are, why is this so? If not, why did you leave? Did you find a substitute?

Reading list

The concepts of reward and costs are essentially economic ideas but have been adapted for social psychology as part of exchange theory. Much more has been written about rewards than costs.

Baron, R.S., Kerr, N. and Miller, N. (1991). *Group Process, Group Decision, Group Action*. Open University Press: Buckingham. The costs of group membership are covered briefly on pp. 2–3 and 122 as part of a discussion about exchange theory. Rewards, as usual, are covered more fully than costs.

Feldman, R.A. and Wodarski, J.S. (1975). *Contemporary Approaches to Group Treatment*. Jossey-Bass: San Francisco, CA. Rewards and costs are covered briefly in terms of exchange theory and the ideas of Thibaut and Kelly (1959: *The Social Psychology of Groups*. John Wiley: New York, pp. 146, 188).

Collins, B.E. and Guetzkow, H. (1964). *A Social Psychology of Group Processes for Decision Making*. John Wiley: New York. This valuable text covers group decision-making and contains a great deal of material about rewards, including the effects they have on group performance and on the satisfaction of members.

9 Affecting group outcomes: working in groups

Introduction

This chapter attempts to put to use the learning which has been gained about groups in terms of deploying actions directed at affecting what a group does. It starts by looking at influence factors and then goes on to look at democracy, knowing what kind of change is required, the basic need for detailed observation, areas to which change efforts can be directed and the gambits which can be used. Lastly, we look briefly at the ethics of intervention.

Up to this point we have attempted to clarify the kind of influences at work in groups and how they can move groups in various directions. By knowing that these influences exist and by being able to recognize them, it is possible to bring pressure to bear upon them in selected ways and in targeted areas either to intensify, diminish, change, avoid or stop them, and in that way the progress of the group can be altered significantly.

So what we are about to look at is how deliberate change can be achieved by group members. In so doing, we will be concerned not only with actions designed to bring about change, but also with ideas of democracy, of choice and the ethical factors involved in the use of knowledge and understanding to bring about change. But let us look for a moment at how the influence factors work and how change is effected in a group using understanding of how groups work and without threatening any member's survival or drastically increasing their costs.

Example

The staff group of a residential centre was meeting to discuss matters relating to the local authority's proposal to change the focus of the group's work by adding day-care facilities. The staff group comprised old hands, relatively new members, both young and older people, full-time and part-time workers, males and females. Some members of the group showed resistance to the proposed change but others were more enthusiastic; however, all of them were somewhat anxious about what the changes would mean in practical terms (e.g. the shift system, extra work, etc.).

The head of the home was an experienced manager and a keen groupworker. Watching this meeting, I was impressed by the way she created time and space for every staff member to say what they felt about the situation. Some just expressed resentment about the lack of consultation, others shrugged their shoulders and remarked that this was typical of management. But gradually what began to emerge was that all the staff members were beginning to realize that there was a considerable diversity of response to the proposed changes and while some scoffing and poking fun took place, there was a slow movement towards modifying their own needs and demands to accommodate the needs and demands of others. Each individual's behaviour was being subtly influenced by their growing perception of the behaviour of others. There was one member who vowed she would not accept any such change, but who was eventually persuaded by the giving of concessions by others who valued her experience.

At the end of the session, nearly everyone had changed their original position – some more than others. But however tentative their new positions were, they all felt that they had been involved in deciding their future work patterns; they all felt that the process had been fair, and although they all accepted that they had been influenced by their colleagues, no-one felt they had been unduly pressed. One middle-aged member commented that it was a pity senior management did not discuss changes in the same way.

This meeting has all the essentials of what working in and with groups is all about (i.e. the control and management of influence to promote certain ends). When several people gather together, the very fact of being aware of the presence of others modifies the behaviour of each individual in subtle and not so subtle ways. Sometimes that awareness of the presence of others and of their expectations can influence individual behaviour to a great extent. Extreme examples of this have been made public by quasi-religious cults, including those of Charles Manson and the Branch Davidian cult of David Koresh.

Working well in groups is concerned with understanding how this awareness of the presence of others and of their expectations influences behaviour, and how that understanding can be used to ensure that the influence factors produce chosen outcomes, which are beneficial in kind. So let us now look at the ways in which our knowledge of group influences can be used in this way to affect group outcome. We start by looking at the idea of democracy.

Democracy

There are always some people in an organization who believe that things would be better if the system operated in line with their own ideas. Therefore, human organizations do not operate with 100 per cent consensus, except for a remarkably short space of time, and then usually under enormous pressure from some outside threat. One fact about human beings is that they have never been particularly effective at agreeing with one another, even when it was necessary for survival. Compromise often seems to be the best they can achieve.

But we have seen how difference is essential, in that it is the source of new ideas and alternatives, and so compromise may be the best we can hope for. In groups which are small organizations, dissent can loom large, but most dissenters will go along with the majority verdict if it can be shown that the alternatives are worse. Therefore, in any group at anytime, some members will believe that what they have got is good, and there will be those who believe that they have the least worst possible deal. In any case, total agreement at the same high level of satisfaction is a recipe for engendering smugness, self-satisfaction, reduction of effort and stagnation.

> Individuals attempt to change groups because they believe that change will ensure a better deal than the one they have got. Resistance comes from those who believe they already have a good deal or who do not want to commit effort to change.

Ideas into action

While the members of a group may wish to effect change, there is always the very important question of how they will go about it. Often I have heard a group member say, 'I would like to have changed what was happening but I didn't know how to go about it'. Many people have a problem translating ideas of change into action. However, some change-methods are learned early in life, such as displays of anger, withdrawal, the creation of conflict, complaining and ganging-up on others, all of which are effective to some degree or other. But all of these are negative responses which have a basis in achieving desired ends. So we need to look at such methods closely and to add to them the clearly more positive methods of suggestion, offering alternatives, discussion, pointing to consequences, highlighting resources, etc. But first let us look at more general ideas about influencing the course of action a group takes and about the somewhat vexed question of leadership.

Knowing what it is you want to change

In order to affect group outcomes, it is only necessary to be a member of a group and to make some minor contribution. Indeed, it is quite logical to argue that the outcome of a group may well be affected by a member or members who do nothing more than grace the group with their presence. Inertia among group members can be a very powerful influence, because the energy which fuels a group's performance derives in the main from the commitment of group members.

But if we are to consider deliberate and conscious attempts by group members to influence the course a group may be taking, either in terms of what it is seeking to achieve or the methods it uses to proceed, then we must start from the basics. In order to bring about modification or change in a system in a selected way, it is necessary to have some knowledge of the system's mode of functioning and of its current state. This is not meant to imply that affecting group outcomes is wholly a matter of taking over the group and manhandling it in the chosen direction, however beneficially or skilfully this may be done. For although this is a perfectly legitimate option, outcomes are affected by other factors, such as the contribution of information, skill and understanding, the sharing and pooling of resources, the generation of insight into what is happening and the beneficial use of experience. These are leadership actions, however simple they may be or however short their duration.

We need to look at what group texts refer to as 'leadership', by which they nearly always mean what might be called professional or designated leadership. In effect, this usually means a person or persons who have planned and brought into being a group or adapted an existing group like a family, for a specific purpose, usually one of benefit to the group members. But the group literature also makes reference to 'natural' leaders, by which is meant group members who have previous experience of group leadership and/or possess a so-called natural ability to exercise control and power in some group situations. Leaders like these are often described as arising spontaneously within groups in order to meet certain circumstances which face the group. Indeed, the literature goes much further and defines the characteristics which are most likely to be found in a natural leader, stressing factors like charisma, experience, intelligence, etc.

It seems to me that while designated leadership may be crucially important where the characteristics necessary to influence group behaviour are signally not possessed by most of the members of a group, or where in the processes of planning and creating a group they may be required – or for terminating the group – most of the movement which pushes a group towards achieving its goals tends to come from the members who make contributions in the ways suggested earlier. This is exactly what one would expect if it is accepted that groups function as pools of resources. Thus what members stand to gain from the group as individuals comes from what they can collectively put into it. So unless the designated leader of a group is also its major resource, what the main skill of such leaders should be is the ability to create a system which encourages and supports all group members to contribute as much as they can to increase the resources available to the group as a whole.

In many organizations, the post of group leader is a formally recognized position and bears a title (e.g. team leader, manager, head of department, officer in charge, etc.). In hierarchical organizations, such posts are part of the system through which organizational policy is filtered downwards to those who are actually going to implement various parts of it. It should also provide a conduit of ideas, recommendations and information from the implementors upwards to the decision- and policy-making levels of the organization, so that their activities can be founded upon what is really occurring at the points of action. As in specifically created groups, it is the members at these points of action who are potentially able to generate resources and provide feedback. Many large organizations often do not listen with sufficient interest to the information that filters up from below, which is one reason why large organizations tend to be much less efficient than small groups, where feedback is often on a face-to-face basis and its effect upon group behaviour patterns is easily and directly monitored.

So in some ways it is better to avoid the use of the terms 'leader' and 'leadership' unless they are very specifically related to directive behaviour. Not only are they emotionally loaded, but in large areas of group activity their use is misleading. Thus we have to use phrases like 'affecting group outcomes', which is used in the title of this chapter.

It is the business of *all* group members to have some effect on group outcomes, ranging from direct challenge and change to support for what actually exists. But it behoves all members to know and be able to control their efforts at producing these effects, because by not having a real understanding of what they are about, many people have supported outcomes with which they were in some disagreement. It is pertinent to remember that silence is usually interpreted to mean consent.

Leadership

If you are asked to run a group, you will have a very firm foundation on which to develop your leadership skills if you have thoroughly explored your

Table 20 The main objectives of leadership

1. To recognize the complexity of the groupwork task
2. To understand themselves, their position and standing and what they are trying to do
3. Performance is the main criterion by which leaders are judged by group members, and it needs to be compatible with the stated aims of the group
4. To be sensitive to, and aware of, the overall environment in which the group operates
5. To recognize the difference between personal attack and being in receipt of displaced disappointment and hostility from the members about the group's performance
6. To come to terms with access to power
7. To develop effective communicating skills and a sense of time and timing

experiences as a group member. When shopfloor workers become managers, they tend to forget much of what they had previously learned. This means that not only should leadership of a group be based on what being a member is like, but it should also be concerned with the overall functioning of the group. Maintaining distance, in the way we looked at earlier as an essential step in learning to understand what a group is doing, is now no longer just a tool of personal learning, but an essential skill that enables a leader to see what the group is doing *all the time*. This is not in any way to diminish the fact that the leader is an essential group component, with much to offer in that capacity. His or her leadership skills are an extra requirement on top of membership skills.

The move from group member to group leader allows that individual to make use of his or her memories of what it felt like to be a member under the guidance of different leaders, to remember the anxieties, the fear of exposure as being ignorant, and incapable, and how new members were eventually integrated. Together with responsibility for the successful stewardship of the group, the new leader has responsibility for the way in which the group settles to its tasks, deals with its problems and utilizes its resources. Just like the change that was involved in becoming a group member, so another change will be required to become an effective group leader. The new leader will know from past experience the kinds of leadership that are effective and those that are not. S/he will know what s/he feels to be compatible with the kind of person s/he is. The new leader will now know more from having monitored the personal feedback received from his or her fellow group members in different group situations.

The process of acquiring skill and understanding as a group leader is similar to the process that new group members undergo. The process of watching, analysing, recording, consulting, discussing, reflecting, etc., is exactly the same, but the new leader has to extend these areas of 'need to know' to the period before a group is created or adapted to groupwork purposes, to the system in which it lies embedded and to the period immediately after its termination or at selected periods during its life if it is an ongoing group.

The new leader's efforts to understand, guide, succour and control are now much more oriented to the welfare of the group as a whole and somewhat less to the enhancement of personal, individual development. Make no mistake, individual development is still very much involved, but its objective is more intensely and positively directed towards the group as a whole.

Not all good group members make good group leaders. After all, groups are collections of individuals who need one another to a greater or lesser extent in order to perform some particular function or to achieve some designated outcome. Leaders possess no value without groups, though sometimes groups can manage quite well on the shared expertise, knowledge and resources of their members and without any accepted overall leader. The balance which has always been tilted in favour of leaders is perhaps an accident of the historical development of our understanding of how groups function, and due in no small measure to a belief that others may be better qualified to understand what is required. In some circumstances, this is indubitably true, and in such groups the leader is the person who is the major – not the sole – group resource. He or she possesses something which is regarded as essential to the other group *members*. But for many groups, each member is a resource for all the others and the role of the leader is much less important.

So if you find that the extra skills which are required for group leadership and the role in which they are to be practised are not for you, content yourself that good membership – effective, knowledgeable and understanding membership – is what actually produces good groups!

Intervention

Conscious intervention in a group which has much chance of success can only come from a relatively clear understanding of what is happening in the group and what has happened up to the point of intervention. There are three basic criteria to follow when any conscious attempt to influence a group is made by one or more of its members (members in all instances includes those members who have a designated leadership role):

1. It must be abundantly clear that some action is necessary.
2. The individual must know the kind of action which is required and feel that he or she is capable of making it, or of influencing others to take it.
3. He or she must also feel that any risk attached to the taking of the action is worth taking.

If criterion 1 is not applicable, then criteria 2 and 3 should not be considered; likewise, criterion 3 can only be considered if criteria 1 and 2 are deemed applicable. Criterion 1 is of course dependent upon having some idea of what is actually happening in the group, as we saw in Chapter 4. This is largely dependent upon good observation. So let us now explore observation more thoroughly, because if the basis of criterion 1 is ill-founded it is unlikely that the subsequent steps leading up to any attempt to change or modify what the group is doing will be successful.

Observation

As we have referred to this necessary skill in previous chapters, some brief notes and reminders should serve here. First, six basic rules:

1. Learn to watch.
2. Note the relationship between observed behaviour and consequences over both the long and short term.
3. Listen (we discussed content and process earlier).
4. Don't make facile assumptions about causes; interpretation of behaviour is a dangerous process, particularly for those lacking experience.
5. Be patient, time is a most important element in group behaviour. It is not possible to see consequences if early intervention prevents their occurrence.
6. Your main purpose in the group is to be an effective member; observing your own behaviour and that of others is only one part of membership, even if it is crucial.

Observing is difficult enough when that is all one is doing, but point 6 must always be borne in mind.

> What you don't see will still affect the way that the group functions, but you will have no chance of doing anything about it even if you want to.

It is also to be remembered that it is possible that you will know things about the group which you have not seen, as there are sources of sensory information that are not visual in nature. So to be a good observer in a group situation, it is necessary to:

1. Know the kinds of things one is looking for.
2. Train oneself to adapt and modify previously learned 'seeing' behaviour.
3. Know what aspects of behaviour are most likely to attract one's attention.
4. Know reasonably well where any blind spots exist.
5. Know what are the most likely interpretations one is going to place on what one sees and their relative validity.
6. Make allowances for these factors and aim for a better level of objectivity.
7. Work at improving one's observational skills.
8. Where possible and acceptable check out the degree of accuracy of observations with others.

As we shall see later in this chapter, when you observe something you have the choice of making it public or not. Nobody will know what you are thinking or feeling. Behaviour is the only cue we have and most of us are not particularly good at assessing behavioural cues without a great deal of practice, or else with the development of increased sensitivity deriving from urgent need, such as survival. One of the many reasons for observers not saying what they see in a group can be laid at the door of an apparently compelling sense that the responsibility to deal with what has been seen rests with the individual. A second and equally compelling urge to remain silent is the fear of making a fool of oneself or of appearing to be ignorant. A third reason is a fear of being wrong. But in decision-making processes, to say nothing is generally accepted as indicating agreement. In any case, as we have seen, the resources of the group would never emerge if they were not demonstrated by the ways in which members participate in group activities.

If a member does reveal what he or she has observed, then the following are also likely to emerge:

1. Others have significantly different viewpoints about the same thing.
2. A significant amount of sharing has already taken place.
3. A rule of being open may be established.
4. A sense of relief may be felt by other members who would have liked to say something but felt inhibited.
5. The creation of an atmosphere in which the admission of ignorance is an acceptable prelude to finding out.
6. An increase in sincerity, as fear of being foolish is diminished.

Achieving change

Having observed what is going on and having decided that some attempt to change things is necessary, then we must look at the ways in which this may be done and ultimately whether such action is ethical.

The following is a list of ways in which a change in the direction of the group may be made:

1. By changing one's own behaviour to act as a role model for change in others; showing how it can be done.
2. By directing change efforts to key individuals to modify their behaviour and to make visible possible directions and kinds of change.
3. By directing change efforts through sub-groups.
4. By directing change efforts at the whole group, which usually involves influencing the group's decision-making processes.
5. By directing change efforts to significant groups and individuals outside the group who have an interest in, and power to bring about, change within the group.

There are ten possible ways of affecting change:

1. Discussion/argument.
2. Providing information.
3. Exposure of the existing situation.
4. Exposure of the probable consequences of any proposed change.
5. Lobbying to gain support.
6. The exercise of external and/or internal authority, whether delegated or personal (e.g. personal power, charisma, etc.).
7. Achieving consensus.
8. Making comparisons with other similar situations.
9. Negotiation (exchange, bargaining, etc.).
10. Threat (persuasion, coercion, etc.).

Let us now consider each in turn.

Discussion/argument

This implies giving every group member the opportunity to put forward for general consumption their ideas and information, feelings about what the group may have done, is doing and will or should be doing in the future. The presentation of such ideas and information, of ways of proceeding, etc., may contain material which will convince and persuade others and thus secure their backing. But it must be stated that discussion does also imply openness and the ability to listen as well as to talk and to challenge. Argument is a method of endeavouring to select rationally from competing options, not a method of hammering down any opposition, though often the term is used to describe such bullying behaviour. Discussion is time-consuming and is not therefore always appropriate, especially in crisis situations when immediate action is required.

Providing information

As we have already seen, decisions made by a group are based upon the information available at the time the decision was made. So change in what a group does may well be founded in changes in the information available to it. Thus additional material and material of a better quality, more detailed, more accurate and more relevant knowledge of the outcomes of using such material, are all apt to upgrade information as a basis for decision-making. However, a word of caution. Logically, better information should result in better decisions, but the degree of rationality which is applied to information is always tempered by non-rational factors (e.g. where the information came from, the status and esteem of the member who volunteered it, etc.). There are many other factors other than the quality, nature and relevance of information which can affect its consideration. Indeed, for those interested in the non-rational handling of information, I would recommend Raven and Rubin's *Social Psychology: People in Groups* (1976: 415–33). It is also possible that too much information will swamp decision-making and generate stagnation.

Exposure of the existing situation

The basic fact about change which is often overlooked is that it involves two positions, that which is current (A) and that which is new (B). Change is then defined as the difference between A and B. So it is axiomatic that for change to be brought about in an effective way, it is necessary to know the present position. It is a fact that not every member of a group will be aware of that position. Each individual may know part of it, usually that part in which he or she is most interested. But the global view is often incomplete. Thus any attempt to achieve an assessment of the current position has to collect all the bits and pieces from members and assemble them into a whole. This may then be compared with:

1. Where individuals thought they were.
2. What they were actually trying to achieve.
3. How effective their current methods have been.
4. What pressures are now revealed which had previously been ignored (e.g. time, deadlines, etc.).
5. What areas require attention.
6. What changes need to be implemented, if any.

It is possible that no immediate need for change will be uncovered. But in any case, the exercise is worthwhile in its own right because it provides an assessment of progress and an affirmation of the correctness of the group's methods and an agreed platform from which the group can proceed. If change is necessary and the existing situation has been clarified, it is more likely that any change will be relevant and have near universal support.

Exposure of the consequences of change

This is an extremely difficult task to do well. To expose the probable consequences of certain behaviours, decisions and actions carries with it the perception of those involved of being responsible. Now although this is true in the sense that consequences *are* dependent upon action and behaviour, blame seems to attach to the whole business of exposing consequence and so it is often regarded as a hostile act.

But the fact that certain actions can be seen to produce certain consequences is a necessary part of any consideration of choices in decision-making. Of course, consequences in many cases cannot be predicted with accuracy and so decisions may have to be taken based on the assumption that predictions of consequence may be wrong or inaccurate. Frequently, indeed, the major consequences of social actions turn out to be those which were unforeseen.

Nevertheless, the consideration of consequences is still a potent instrument for influencing group process, particularly if the consequences exposed have been overlooked or underestimated in the group's deliberations. The formula goes something like this:

- This is what we propose to do.
- The probable consequences of enacting these proposals will be like this.
- Is this what we want to achieve?

Stated as clearly as this, it often has the effect of causing the group to reconsider, to ask for more information or even to change its approach and sometimes its target.

Lobbying to gain support

This is a power tactic in that it relies on the impression created by numbers and on the power of any members who may be of high standing in the group. It also often contains an element of bargaining. Thus in order to elicit support for ideas and proposals, individual members may have to place themselves under obligation to other members. Efficient lobbying tends to bring about change by virtue of the power which coalitions can exert, in terms of personal power that is charismatic or in the power to reward or punish. The bargaining element is usually based on the currency of support (i.e. you support me now and I will look with favour on any requests for support you require at a later date).

The exercise of authority

Authority is usually seen as power invested in individuals by an organization which has the recognized right to do so. But power may be vested in group members because of their proven record of achievement, or because they have engendered a great liking among their colleagues, or perhaps because it is believed that they possess some relevant expertise. In essence, they are group members whose words and actions count for something and who thus carry other members with them. Thus they are able to instigate change. But perceptions can change and it is possible for the possessors of such authority to lose their standing and their ability to bring about change by example and personal persuasion. If such people possess authority vested in them by a source of power outside of the group, then such a loss of esteem tends to produce a conflict between their designated authority and their loss of group status.

Achieving consensus

The level of agreement necessary between members for a change to be implemented depends to a considerable extent on the formal structure of the group. The decision-making process in groups can range from complete dictatorship to absolute democracy. In different circumstances, either of these extremes may be very relevant, but in most groups consensus is seldom to be equated with total agreement. The wishes of the majority are usually the accepted standard and once they have been ascertained the minority are expected to cooperate. This does not always happen and it is not unknown for determined minorities to cause considerable havoc and sometimes the reversal or amendment of the

(a)

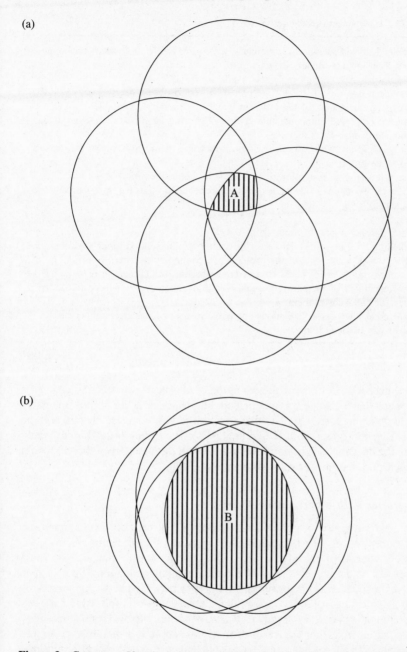

(b)

Figure 3 Consensus. If each circle represents the ideas, attitudes and opinions of each member of a five-member group, then the shaded area A shows where these overlap and thus where the area of consensus and agreement will be. In (a) the group's opinions, etc., are widely divergent and thus the area of consensus is small. If this small area can be made explicit, it can form the basis of minimal agreement and work can begin to increase it if necessary. In (b) all the group members are in substantial agreement and action taken about the area of consensus will find large backing and little dissent.

144 Survival in groups

Table 21 Barriers preventing consensus in groups

1. Hostility between members, particularly when it arises from diametrically opposed views about matters under consideration
2. There are just not enough real facts available to the group
3. Where there are facts they are interpreted in very differing ways
4. There is no clear view of the problem which is generally acceptable
5. There are large and unreconcilable differences in the values, attitudes, prejudices and backgrounds of the members
6. Equally, there are wide rifts in the aims which the members have for themselves and for the group
7. There is inadequate resolution of the conflicts within the group
8. Dislike of the member originating an idea rather than a sincere disagreement about the idea itself

How such barriers might be removed:
1. By dealing with controversial issues in commonly understood terms with the goal of discovering what parts of the problem are commonly accepted (see Fig. 2)
2. Differences between members tend to create barriers which can be reduced by the simple expedient of increasing the knowledge members have of these factors by a process of exposure to them
3. Where good interpersonal relationships exist, many of the barriers either do not arise or can be dealt with

disputed decision. But one of the strengths of consensus in effecting change is not so much that a change is implemented, but that because all or most members were involved in instigating it, there is a significant chance that it will be sustained by the group even if it runs into serious difficulties. This is largely because the decision is *theirs* and was not something forced upon the group and for which they feel no sense of ownership.

Comparisons with other similar situations

This is a favourite ploy of politicians used both to bolster their own policies and to discredit those of others. Indeed, there is great value in being able to offer concrete evidence of the effectiveness of some proposed change. The snag, however, lies in the understanding of the phrase 'similar situation'. Similar does not mean identical, and though certain similarities may exist between two groups to such a degree that it can be decided that a precedent worth following has been found, caution is necessary. Even small dissimilarities may well precipitate very large variations in the consequences of implementation. It is therefore extremely wise when offering comparisons as a guide to a proposed change in group activity, to make explicit the known differences and not to force the comparisons but to make allowances for the differences. Chaos theory has taught a powerful lesson to all scientists that even small differences in what are called 'initial conditions' can produce large variations in outcome.

But if other people have done most of the spade work in setting up the kind of change a group wishes to bring about, there is no great value in repeating all that labour if it can be used elsewhere with suitable caution. Finally, comparison tends to reduce the fear element of any change; others have done it or something like it, so it should be safe.

Negotiation

This change strategy is implicit in several of the others. Fundamentally, it involves the idea of exchange or bargain, plus compromise. Negotiation has been described as the process by which nobody gets everything they wanted but everybody gets something. The way it proceeds depends entirely upon the perceptions of those involved of the bargaining strengths held by others and upon the degree of importance of the focus of the negotiations. The process involves not just information, ideas, beliefs, etc., but also time, value systems, concepts of rights and duties, and advantage and disadvantage.

Threat

All change implies some form of threat. Indeed, it is often said that the greatest obstacle to change is the threat it offers to stable current practice. The costs of change are usually assessed in terms of loss of that stability, in terms of the increase in energy required to effect change, a belief that the outcome will not be worth it, a loss of routine and of privilege, and so on. Nevertheless, another form of threat is frequently used as a change agent, which is to point out the consequences of non-compliance. This can take the form of expulsion from the group or of various reductions in status and power.

Persuasion, coercion and the threats of punishment or reward are common factors in attempts to instigate change. They are similar in that an element of fear is involved. We considered the difference between public conformity and private acceptance earlier, and it must be obvious here that the use of coercion as an instrument of change falls largely in the area of the production of public conformity. As such, although change may be brought about, it is dependent upon the continued existence of the threat which was present at its inception. Should perception of the value of that threat diminish, then in all likelihood the changes based on it will disintegrate.

There is to some extent an overlap between the above ten ways of effecting change. All change strategies are concerned with convincing others that change is necessary in their terms, that it is possible and that the rewards will ultimately exceed the costs. These three factors are essential. Many changes are seen by groups as extremely desirable, but if they are also seen either as not easy to obtain or only to be bought at great cost, or both, then no attempt will be made to effect them. We must never forget that:

> Change implies threat, increased effort and risk

and also that unless perceived rewards exceed perceived costs by a reasonable
amount, change will not take place.

Ethics of intervention

Change may be perceived as beneficial for the group, but all group members
have a right to refuse to take part in it even if their refusal causes a marked
deterioration in the situation of the group. All that may be attempted legitimately
is to ascertain that what is proposed is fully understood and the consequences
of acceptance and rejection are equally clearly understood without any imputa-
tion of blame or threat (see 'Exposure of the consequence of change' above).

People are often required to make choices between apparent options when in
effect no choice exists, largely because the nature of the options and thus the
consequence of choice are not understood. This is a difficult situation, because
no-one likes to appear ignorant in public, especially when others appear to understand, and so selection is made not rationally but under some fear of exposure.

In this context, explanation is seldom adequate unless some indication of
understanding other than facile acceptance is apparent. The question, 'Do you
understand?', is frequently useless; but the request, 'Tell me what you understand by this in your own words', can provide a demonstration of whether an
individual does understand something, and the nature, quality and extent of that
understanding.

It may on occasions be necessary to compel people to change; it may ultimately prove to have been for their benefit and they may come to see and accept
this. The process therefore may have changed from one of conformity to one of
acceptance – but always acceptance based upon a true understanding of what is
involved. Gaining consent – that is, requesting and being given a mandate to
pursue certain actions and to make decisions – is a time-consuming and frustrating procedure and the temptation may arise to take short cuts, ignore dissent and
force the issue. Even when the result of such action turns out to have been
necessary and beneficial, the dramatic changes which ensue in group morale are
seldom positive and are almost always long-lasting, having deleterious effects
upon future decision-making situations.

Summary of main points

- Intended change in groups can be successfully achieved when based upon a
  clear understanding of what is required.

- Change efforts are leadership acts, however small or limited in duration.
- Leadership is a complex skill which can often be developed from competent membership abilities.
- There are techniques and strategies for creating change which can be learned. But knowing what they are needs to be developed by practice into actions which stand some chance of being successful.
- Intervention with deliberate intent to influence group outcomes needs to be based in sound ethical judgement, especially of consequence.

Basic concepts and terms

These are indicated in the text, so that what needs to be emphasized here is the 'ideas-into-action' problem. Transferring thoughts into patterns of behaviour is something that many people find difficult. It requires conscious effort and as much assisted practice as possible.

Topics for discussion

1. Take any two of the ten forms of achieving change and explain why and how each can be used to bring about change in what a group achieves. If possible, give examples from your own experience.
2. Record your feelings about watching people, particularly if those you are watching know you are doing it.
3. How do you think you would explain observing what is going on in a group to its members if they asked you?

Reading list

Nearly all groupwork texts contain large sections on leadership, so there is little need to give specific reading on that topic here.

Northen, H. (1969). *Social Work with Groups*. Columbia University Press: New York. Like most North American writers of the period on groupwork, Northen pays attention to democratic concepts. The text is worth reading for a clear, unfussy exposition of 'democratic' groupwork.

Douglas, T. (1976). *Groupwork Practice*. Tavistock: London. This is a very practical text on working with groups. It is very leadership-oriented but with good material on observation.

Milson, F. (1975). *An Introduction to Group Work Skills*. Routledge and Kegan Paul: London. This is another practical text with chapters on observation, action and leadership. The text is based largely on Youth Club experience.

Garvin, C.D. (1981). *Contemporary Groupwork*. Prentice Hall: Englewood Cliffs, NJ. The author comes from an American school of groupwork devoted to planning strategic approaches to working with groups. Thus Chapters 5, 6 and 7 are concerned with the methods and techniques of achieving change in groups through operations at different levels of group structure.

Raven, B.H. and Rubin, J.Z. (1976). *Social Psychology: People in Groups*. John Wiley: New York. This book contains a good discussion of the problems of the non-rational handling of information.

10 Learning from experience

Necessary groupwork knowledge

Formal training in groupwork is not readily available in the UK, so this chapter presents ways in which a self-learning programme can be constructed based on personal effort and experience. The material covers what groupworkers need to know and learning without supervision, which is broken down into ten areas in which effort can be made.

As long ago as 1959, Kadushin listed the following as the knowledge he deemed necessary for a groupworker to possess. He was considering workers operating as group leaders, but as we have already seen most of this knowledge is also essential for the effective group member:

The group worker needs to know something about:

1. The history and development of groupwork agencies.
2. The functions they currently serve in the community.
3. The structure of groupwork agencies.
4. The administration of such agencies.

5. The relationship of the agency to:
   - the neighbourhood,
   - other social agencies,
   - non-social work community agencies.
6. How to differentiate groupwork function from recreation or adult education.
7. The nature and variety of groups that are likely to use such agencies.
8. The process of formation of such groups.
9. Group cohesion; group morale; leadership; interaction; control; subgroup formation; the effects of cliques, pairs, isolates; status structure; decision-making; contagion; differential group roles; rejection/acceptance patterns in groups.
10. Skill in:
    (a) developing program activities,
    (b) leading program activities,
    (c) helping groups plan program activities.
11. The activities appropriate for each age level and the patterns of association at each age level.
12. The effect on individuals of differentiated activities and processes.
13. The skills in helping the individual to use the group constructively.

Some of Kadushin's points need examination for our current purposes, viz. all group members who are interested in working in and with groups of people need to have some understanding of the system in which any particular group is embedded. For instance, a care worker would need to have some understanding not just of the organization of the care centre, but also of the social organization of which it was a part. Now this often seems to people in day care and residential care to be none of their business, but they are wrong. As we have seen, the larger system in which a group operates can, and often does, have a significant influence on the way individual units within its boundaries can function. In the other direction, successful *and* disastrous units create spin-off effects for the larger system. For our purposes, the most important consideration is that it is basically extremely wasteful of scarce resources to attempt to establish a group or work with existing groups in such a way that the larger system will not bear. This is not to say that new ideas should never be tried, quite the contrary, but they should all start from a true consideration of what is already in existence and how it can be used as a basis to move on to different things. All change tends to generate some anxiety and this sometimes fuels resistance. Where an understanding of the larger system exists, then it is possible to use that knowledge to introduce at appropriate times, at the right level and to the right people the kind of changes that are proposed and also with the correct amount of difference which will not make acceptance difficult.

Where no understanding of how groups fit into the larger system exists, there is a very distinct possibility that behaviour which appears in the group will be attributed to influences which exist entirely within it. But as we have seen, some of the most potent influences operating within a group exist outside of it. Indeed, when membership of a particular group represents only a very small part of an individual's life, then each member will bring to each group session he or she attends a considerable degree of baggage (e.g. preoccupation, consideration, involvement, etc.), which relates not to the group as such but to life outside of it.

The whole basis of Kadushin's list, which is concerned to demonstrate the range and depth of knowledge which he considers essential to the development of understanding about how groups function, is entirely compatible with the main theses of this book. It points up the need to broaden one's perceptions to include possibilities that are not immediately obvious, to be prepared for eventualities whose causes may lie outside the group. The methods available to achieve this kind of breadth of knowledge and skill are as follows:

1. Taking a full- or part-time course in groupwork.
2. Receiving competent supervision while being a member of a group.
3. Wide reading on groups and groupwork and social behaviour.
4. Analysing one's personal group experience.
5. Consultation and discussion with others.

Learning without supervision

What should be evident to the reader by now is the fact that not a great deal of help is available to those who want to learn about working in and with groups. Granted there are courses which cover the theoretical concepts of group behaviour. There are also courses which pursue an essentially selective method of working with groups, which exacts adherence to a particular theoretical line. There are also courses which are oriented to the practice of groupwork in very specific settings and with potential group members who have particular problems, difficulties or needs. Thus it is possible to find instruction on functioning in a committee, in group therapy and in, say, groups of people who have been sexually abused as children. But it is extremely difficult to obtain any satisfactory instruction, both theoretical and practical, in the ways of successful survival and participation in the groups in which most of us spend a considerable part of our lives – work groups, friendship groups, leisure activity groups, families, neighbourhood communities, etc. – the groups which form the fabric of our society. It is equally hard for those whose work is concerned with caring for others to receive adequate help in developing the necessary skills.

Given this situation, any aspiring learner is faced with the daunting prospect of devising a self-learning programme which includes as much outside consultation and discussion as can be acquired by fair means or foul. This chapter will present some of the techniques of designing a self-learning programme about working with groups, which starts from the basic assumption that any individual is already a member of several social groups.

> The raw material of a self-learning programme on working in groups comes from the learner's experience of groups of which he or she is already a member.

Self-help programmes

The techniques involved in the creation of a self-help programmes are as follows:

1. Distancing oneself.
2. Consultation – comparison with others.
3. Recording – accumulation and organization of experience.
4. Reflection – clarifying experiences by thinking about them.
5. Feedback – attending to response patterns.
6. Monitoring – evaluating success and failure.
7. Trying out – deliberately using what has been learned.
8. Reading – relating experience to the recorded experience of others.
9. Self-understanding – realizing individual potential and limitations.
10. Supervision – where it is available.

Distancing oneself

The first factor involved in the creation of a self-help programme is rather different from usual. Normally, people accept that they are members of groups, some of which like the family they have no choice in being a member. Others they choose to enter in order to achieve specific ends, drift into, join to please someone else or are curious, etc. There are myriad reasons why people join or find themselves members of groups, but the main reason is that the form of work an individual does to earn a living more often than not establishes the individual as part of an organization, and therefore they work in the presence of others with a greater or lesser degree of intensity, of dependence and of interrelatedness. In a word, they work in a group.

In order to learn what is available from membership of such groups, it becomes essential to place that membership outside of oneself and to look at the experience as if one is watching a film of that experience. This is not entirely possible, because the greater the meaning a group has in one's life, the more difficult it is to stand apart from it and to regard it dispassionately. But it should be stated that the intensity of involvement in a group has to be matched by a greater effort to withdraw from the group temporarily in order to see the group as a whole as a functioning unit.

In order to understand how a group functions as a total unit, a group member has temporarily to put distance between his or her involvement in that group and him or herself.

Individual members of a group quite naturally tend to look at the group in terms of what he or she gains from membership, and thus the way the group functions is thought of as it effects each individual. This can blind individuals to the effect the group may be having on others and even more importantly how the group as a total unit is operating. For instance, several members of a group may express themselves satisfied with the group and quite content for it to continue in its present form. They may be wholly unaware that other members are experiencing different degrees of satisfaction and dissatisfaction with all or with parts of the group process. This is normal and occurs in all groups throughout their lifespan. However, such disparities in satisfaction can diminish the effectiveness of the group to a marked degree, even to the point of causing it to disintegrate. One principal result of such disparity is that the group provides less satisfaction for *all* its members. But in order to reduce disparity its presence has first to be recognized by all the members of the group and then some decision has to be made about what, if anything, can be done.

Such recognition is only possible when the group as a whole is viewed from some emotional distance. Let us take an example of this kind of distancing in operation. Most groups make decisions which tend to be based upon what at first appears to be a very simple procedure. For example:

1. A situation arises which requires attention.
2. Some of the members of the group recognize that such a situation exists.
3. They discuss their feelings with the group as a whole.
4. When the membership as a whole has been made aware of the situation, they may realize that some decision is required, even if that means doing nothing.
5. The group then discuss the situation to define precisely what it is.
6. Proposals for dealing with the situation are then discussed.
7. From the discussion, certain proposals appear to be more acceptable than others.
8. These proposals may then be voted on or accepted by virtue of the lack of opposition to them.
9. The practical aspects of implementing the proposals are arranged.
10. The proposals are implemented.
11. The effects of implementation are monitored and if further changes are required, the proposal procedure is repeated.

Most people recognize the validity of this step-by-step procedure, yet few members of groups questioned immediately after this decision-making process has been gone through have any clear idea of how the decisions the group has

made were arrived at. Why? The answer is quite simple. It only takes a degree
of individual involvement in the process of group decision-making, especially if
it is a matter of personal concern, for the actual process while it is occurring to
slide completely out of focus.

Consider the following. You are a group member and you are arguing for the
acceptance by the group of a change in policy about admitting new members.
What you need to concentrate on is presenting your argument and thinking
furiously about how to put your points across. What will be unclear is how those
members of the group who are taking little active part in the debate are thinking.

It is important to observe how the group as a whole responds to what is
happening if the processes by which a group makes decisions is to stand
revealed.

It will be remembered from our discussion on being able to influence group
outcomes that nothing influential can be done which is not based upon a clear
understanding of what is happening in the group. The basis of acquiring the skill
to know what is happening lies in practising distancing oneself from the actual
group.

Exercise

In one of the groups of which you are a member, there must be times
when you feel there is no great need for a herculean effort on your part to
help the group achieve its goals. This is an ideal opportunity to learn.
Pretend that instead of being a long-standing member you have been invited
by the group to give it feedback on how it performs its various functions –
and then *watch*. See how suggestions are made and whether they are
influential or simply ignored, what kind of responses are made (gestural as
well as verbal) and what the consequences are. If some crisis – great or
small – arises which requires you to resume full membership responsibility,
it will not be difficult to change gear, and what you will have witnessed may
well be of inestimable value to the group in the long run. Finally, you should
record for your own personal satisfaction and learning exactly what you saw
during your time as observer.

Consultation

By consultation I do not mean referring to some high-powered expert, but merely
that as progress is made in learning about groups and experience is gained about
taking action in groups, all this material should be talked over with some person
who is prepared to listen. There is no real requirement that such a person should
know a great deal about groups; if they do, so much the better. The primary
purpose is to engage in an exercise which compels the verbal expression of

cumulative experience, and the need to formulate problems and difficulties in a lucid way so that the hearer is able to understand. Often, the very fact of having to verbalize what may have been vague clarifies and increases understanding even before any feedback from the hearer is received.

The process of consultation is often described as using another person, with less involvement in the same group issues, as a soundboard. One of the great values of groups is that a group constitutes several soundboards, and to explore one's ideas and experiences for increased understanding and clarity with just one person can also increase an individual's awareness of how the process operates in groups. It is of course eminently possible to use the group in a consultation exercise, providing that its members are willing.

Recording

However much it is stressed that recording what goes on in a group is a tool of personal development as well as a means of recording the life of a group, it is a ploy regarded with great antipathy by even professional groupworkers. But whether the recording is elaborate, time-related and detailed, or merely the briefest of notes of the sequence of the major events, the logic of it as a learning instrument is quite simple and direct. What goes on in a group is complex and it is impossible to remember in any great detail the sequence of events of a group session after it has ended. Also, there are usually long time intervals between sessions. Each session starts with some members recalling how the last one ended. Thus events which occur in a later session may well be influenced, if not caused, by events occurring in much earlier sessions. As our intent as workers with groups is to use our understanding of groups to facilitate the achievement of members' aims, it is common sense that some aid to memory, some help in noting sequences and patterns over relevant periods of time, needs to be available to counter any distortions and losses of memory. If records are not kept, then not only will we miss much of value and make many avoidable errors, but our learning about our group competence will also be deficient. For instance, we may have no recollection of the actions taken in the group and thus no method of assessing the actual value of those actions. As in any other kinds of action, learning to do better has to be based upon an analysis of the effectiveness of actions already taken, which will then permit us to amend any observed deficiencies, inaccuracies and outright mistakes.

Reflection

This is a process of quite simply going over in one's mind what one has actually experienced and endeavouring to trace connections between events, actions and feelings. People often say at the end of the working day that they are glad to leave it behind them; therefore, they have no desire to mull over what has happened during the day. So be it, but all the processes of learning, particularly when they concern an activity with such complexity as being in a group, require an ability to see the consequences of events in order to establish the degree of effectiveness of any actions taken. If reflection does not take place, then the development of understanding will remain at a relatively basic level, and mistakes will continue to be made and opportunities missed because the connection between cause and effect will not have been well established. There is a strong connection between how much reflection on group events takes place and the level of commitment and interest in the group and its activities.

Feedback

This method of learning is based upon deliberately looking for and consciously requiring comment upon how an individual or group is working. It has active and passive forms. In the active form, an individual will seek comments on his or her performance in the group from the group members. This has to be done with a degree of caution because comment can hurt, especially if it does not coincide with expectation. Therefore, it is better to be sure that comment is what an individual actually wants or to restrict it to areas with which that individual can cope and as far as possible to be sure that the group atmosphere is a supportive one. Specific individuals can be chosen to give feedback on performance rather than the group as a whole if this seems to be more relevant to the situation.

Passive feedback is not really passive, but the term implies that it is a process which the individual member instigates without the direct involvement of others. It means that there is a deliberate intent to note reactions which will tend to indicate how an individual is seen by others. The problem of this method is that the feedback is monitored through the individual's idiosyncratic perception and does not have the advantage of comparison with the perceptions of others.

It is well to remember that the efficient performance of any system or organization is dependent to a large extent upon the quality and quantity of feedback it receives and ultimately on the use that it makes of that feedback.

Monitoring

This implies keeping a record of what happens and watching to see the connections between events and persons. Short-term monitoring – say over the period of one session – becomes cumulatively long-term monitoring over the lifespan of the group. If monitoring does not take place, there is a strong tendency to see events in a group as single entities. But this is very short-sighted. All events are part of a sequence, which means there are what are called 'antecedents' (i.e. other events which lead up to a situation) and there are 'consequences' which follow an event. No group event can be given its true value in the life of the group if its antecedents and consequences are ignored. Some antecedent events are precipitative (i.e. they actually trigger another event), some are causative (i.e. they are the origins of the event), while others are merely antecedent in that they occurred earlier in time than the event under consideration.

Monitoring, watching and recording make it possible to observe, sometimes over a considerable time-span, the complete sequence of which one particular group event was a part. From this can emerge a much truer picture of the nature of that event.

Trying out

When you believe that you have begun to understand some of the ways in which a group of which you are a member actually operates, then it is time to try to turn that understanding into action. There is a world of difference between understanding in the privacy of one's own head and actually exploiting that understanding by doing something. For instance, you may have discovered that in your work group new ideas are seldom accepted if they are put forward as bald statements of opinion, but that new ideas can be presented and accepted for consideration if they are put forward as part of general conversation, when their nature is partly obscured. So now you have to try to present a new idea to the group and deliberately use what you know. This is not deceit. If you want to give it a name, it is using the system. If the ideas put forward are seen to be of benefit to the group as a whole, it is better that they should at least be considered – after all, if they are not heard their value for the group will never be tested.

Once understanding has been submitted to the test of action, then the kind of 'knowing' it represents is significantly different and offers an extra confidence to the knower. It also becomes cumulative as more and more understandings are tested against actions based on them.

Reading

It goes without saying that all those who wish to learn about groups should read as widely as possible. There are many different approaches and ideas on offer and thus the possibility of some confusion. Make sure that you know the viewpoint of each writer because he or she may be trying to sell you a particular line. There is no harm in this at all; naturally, if something works well for the writer, he or she will want to share that with others. But it is essential to have some idea of whether it is relevant for your particular needs. If you find good ideas, then try to put them into practice. There are many excellent ideas, but that doesn't mean that they will necessarily work for you. As you will have gathered, the resources of a group spring from significant differences between members and this may well preclude some individuals being compatible or comfortable with particular ideas.

Most texts on groupwork are directed at people who are group leaders and are often concerned with particular theoretical concepts. For these reasons, it should be possible to find a text which appeals and which can therefore be used as the starting point and a stepping stone to other texts. (A short reading list will be found at the end of this chapter.)

Self-understanding

If, as has been supposed here, learning about groups and how to work with them and in them has to be based on self-learning, then one of the more essential elements must be an increase in self-knowledge. This does not mean a complex analysis, but it does imply an increase in awareness of blind spots, areas of moderate ability and strengths. One of the first areas of exploration should be to discover the individual's dominant learning mode. For example, some people learn best by talking about what they are doing, some by reading, some by writing, others have to draw diagrams or make lists, others need to be involved in actions. One of these approaches usually sits more comfortably than the others, and when an individual discovers which it is, it should become as far as possible the preferred mode of learning. This does not mean abandoning the others, but it does mean that the most important areas of a central core of knowledge need to be approached in the dominant mode to achieve maximum effect for minimum effort.

Because group members constitute the elements of which a group system is composed and thus become the centre and focus of interaction, it is necessary that they should begin to learn rather more about themselves than is ordinarily customary. Prejudice, ignorance, temper, bias, humour and understanding are neither good nor bad in themselves, but the effects they can produce both for the individual and the group should actually be known if an increase in relative objectivity is to be developed and a correspondingly clearer understanding of group process is to be achieved.

Supervision

The best way of developing the skills of membership and of understanding groups is to experience supervision by a skilled groupwork supervisor. There is no substitute for the feedback that can be obtained from a competent supervisor, deriving either from shared experience in the same group or from the learner's experience related to and discussed with such a supervisor. But such experience is difficult to come by and its value tends to be underrated by many who wish to learn. Perhaps the best that many can obtain is to be a member or even a co-leader in a group which is primarily concerned with understanding how a group works.

Exercises

As the reader will have noted, very few exercises are given in this book. This is because the real value of any exercises designed to facilitate performance in, and understanding of, group behaviour is that they should be performed in groups, whereas the main thrust of this book has been to encourage the individual who is already a multi-group member to understand how groups work and how they can be influenced. Thus the book is directed at individuals in the hope that they can develop its contents to form an individual learning programme. It would, therefore, be somewhat invidious to include a series of exercises which, while wholly appropriate to a group training programme, would be of little value to an individual who did not have a learning group in which they could be used.

However, for those people who are able to introduce exercises into a group for the purpose of learning directly about group behaviour, there are many books which have lists of exercises. But because their exercises are part of a very competent text on groups and groupwork, I believe the exercises in Napier and Gershenfeld (1973) would form an excellent starting point. Another book which offers group exercises to members and leaders for developing proficiency in group participation is *Group Participation: Techniques for Leaders and Members* (Bertcher 1979).

Working in groups

Learning is an active and positive pursuit. As we noted in Chapter 1, learning can take place just by being exposed to situations which compel some interest and a need to participate. But unless such experience is considered as raw material and processed and structured, it will not produce its maximum potential value.

What this book has attempted to do is to provide information about groups and about the information and skills necessary to be a good group member and an effective leader when necessary. It also provides stimulus and direction for the reader to engage actively in the process of learning by doing things, by testing out ideas in real life. There is an enormous gap between knowing (or in some cases believing) and doing, and it is only the determination of the individual learner to commit energy to the learning process which will actually bridge it.

Tom Lehrer, an American academic and entertainer, once said: 'Life is like a sewer, what you get out of it depends on what you put into it'. While the analogy is not strictly true, the general intent is absolutely correct.

One final point is that although the ideas offered here will provide a lead to the process of active learning, they are neither complete nor specifically adapted to each individual learner. Thus a major part of the learning process is for the learner to use his or her creative imagination to adapt and to devise compatible methods and techniques. However, it must be remembered that one of the major aids to learning is to make a simple record of what has been attempted, how it turned out and what yet needs to be done. As we have already noted, change is only measurable between two known points in time. This means assessment and recording at the earliest point in time to form a baseline against which change can be measured. Memory is seldom adequate for this purpose, particularly if the time gap between two points is great, because individuals suffer from distortions and losses of memory.

The opportunity to study groups is all around us in all aspects of daily life. This allows otherwise inexplicable behaviour to be seen as related to group effects rather than to solely individual personality factors. Working with people in groups provides the opportunity to put the cumulative result of observation, knowledge and action to positive use, with an increased efficiency which should be beneficial to all.

Summary of main points

This chapter has described the methods and strategies which are available to create a learning programme in situations where little or no outside help is available. It has been stressed that such a learning programme requires a great deal of effort, discipline and application to be effective. Self learners are responsible to no-one but themselves for their progress or lack of it.

List of basic concepts and terms

Distancing oneself: physically distancing oneself from a group in order to be able to consider it more objectively.

Consultation: the process of discussing with an uninvolved person the ideas, understanding and difficulties which have been encountered during group experiences.

Recording: keeping a record of what has happened in a group to enable a better understanding of how the group's patterns are built up.

Reflection: a process of recalling group activities; a process of attempting to visualize in tranquillity the complex and often turbulent behaviour of a group and if possible to recall it in sequence.

Feedback: receiving and using comment and response to become more aware of the effect one is having on others.

Monitoring: really a more precise form of reflecting, in that a particular process in the group is pursued, sometimes over a long period of time, in order to see the whole process through to its ultimate outcome.

Trying out: as ideas about how groups function are acquired, they need to be converted to actions and deliberately initiated to find out whether they work.

Reading: many good ideas and much general understanding about group membership can be found in texts, but they do need to be tried out and personalized.

Self-understanding: a broadening of the way we understand how we come across to others is essential for members of groups.

Supervision: a form of apprenticeship to a competent groupworker is by far the best way of learning.

Topics for discussion

1. Have you discovered yet what is your most effective mode of learning? If not, why not?
2. Have you made some notes on what has happened recently in one of the groups of which you are a member? If you have, look at them in sequence:
   • Do they show patterns of behaviour?
   • Do these patterns extend over several sessions?

- Can you discern where some of the major events started?
- What were the eventual outcomes?
3. Take a group you know well and write a brief summary of how it works.

Reading list

Bertcher, H.J. (1979). *Group Participation: Techniques for Leaders and Members*. Sage Publications: London.

Priestley, P., McGuire, J., Flegg, D., Hemsley, V. and Welham, D. (1978). *Social Skills and Personal Problem Solving: A Handbook of Methods*. Tavistock: London. This book is not specifically about groups and groupwork. Nevertheless, it is about working with people and it does demonstrate ways of improving social skills which are appropriate to working in groups. It is essentially very practical and should be dipped into for ideas.

Benson, J.F. (1987). *Working More Creatively with Groups*. Tavistock: London. This book, about being a group leader, is written by a practising groupworker. It is packed with ideas about planning and setting up a group, running it and is designed for learners as much as experienced groupworkers. There are many summaries, charts and tables and much practical wisdom.

Brown, A. and Clough, R. (eds) (1989). *Groups and Groupings: Life and Work in Day and Residential Centres*. Tavistock/Routledge: London. The contributors to this book cover groups in residential and day-care centres, family centres, a mental health clinic, a probation hostel, IT, homes for the mentally handicapped and the family. Thus it is an excellent reference for those working with groups in these particular settings. Chapters 2 and 11 also present theoretical ideas of value and a framework for practice.

Douglas, T. (1976). *Groupwork Practice*. Tavistock: London. This is a wide-ranging, general text on the leadership of groups. It has collected together a large amount of material from many different sources, and offers charts, checklists and easily read information about many different kinds of groups. There is also a glossary and an annotated reading list (somewhat out of date now, but still useful). The chapter on observing is of special interest.

Kadushin, A. (1959). The knowledge base of social work, in A.J. Kahn (ed.) *Issues in American Social Work*, pp. 33–9. Columbia University Press: New York. Some 40–50 years ago American social work was concerned with defining the theoretical basis of the profession. This is one of the most concise efforts at doing so, and demonstrates the vast area which social workers believed they should know about. In fact such large borrowings could only be superficially learnt and used, and indeed this approach actually encouraged the development and adoption of a very narrow and highly specialized knowledge base as a reaction.

Napier, R.W. and Gershenfeld, M.K. (1973). *Groups: Theory and Experience.* Houghton Mifflin: Boston, MA. This American text provides a good general survey of working with groups, but more especially gives many exercises designed to aid the performance of groupworkers. The idea of leadership put forward here is that of facilitator and this should be remembered when reading the book.

Raven, B.H. and Rubin, J.Z. (1976). *Social Psychology: People in Groups.* John Wiley: New York. As the title indicates, this is an American text on social psychology, which is very easy to read and is packed with information and research about social behaviour. Chapters 7–10 are specifically concerned with groups – not groupwork, but what is generally understood to happen in groups of all kinds. This is an expensive book and perhaps best consulted through a library.

Index